ISBN 978-0-364-57477-5
PIBN 11275999

This book is a reproduction of an important historical work. Forgotten Books uses state-of-the-art technology to digitally reconstruct the work, preserving the original format whilst repairing imperfections present in the aged copy. In rare cases, an imperfection in the original, such as a blemish or missing page, may be replicated in our edition. We do, however, repair the vast majority of imperfections successfully; any imperfections that remain are intentionally left to preserve the state of such historical works.

1 MONTH OF FREE READING

at

www.ForgottenBooks.com

By purchasing this book you are eligible for one month membership to ForgottenBooks.com, giving you unlimited access to our entire collection of over 1,000,000 titles via our web site and mobile apps.

To claim your free month visit:
www.forgottenbooks.com/free1275999

English
Français
Deutsche
Italiano
Español
Português

www.forgottenbooks.com

Mythology Photography **Fiction**
Fishing Christianity **Art** Cooking
Essays Buddhism Freemasonry
Medicine **Biology** Music **Ancient**
Egypt Evolution Carpentry Physics
Dance Geology **Mathematics** Fitness
Shakespeare **Folklore** Yoga Marketing
Confidence Immortality Biographies
Poetry **Psychology** Witchcraft
Electronics Chemistry History **Law**
Accounting **Philosophy** Anthropology
Alchemy Drama Quantum Mechanics
Atheism Sexual Health **Ancient History**
Entrepreneurship Languages Sport
Paleontology Needlework Islam
Metaphysics Investment Archaeology
Parenting Statistics Criminology
Motivational

Historic, Archive Document

Do not assume content reflects current scientific knowledge, policies, or practices.

WHOLESALE.

THE PRICES WE QUOTE IN THIS LIST ARE ABOUT THE SAME AS THOSE GIVEN TO THE TRADE BY WHOLESALE JOBBERS.

THIS BOOK TELLS WHERE TO BUY
Best Seed for the Least Money

1896.

WARRANTED NORTHERN GROWN SEED.

SEED CATALOGUE

J. J. BELL,

BINGHAMTON,

New York.

BULBS, TREES, PLANTS, ETC.

Our Business:

Being largely growers, we can sell direct to the planters for cash as cheap as a jobber can sell to the dealers, on time.

We can issue a list of seeds, like this one, and mail it direct to planters for about two cents each, while the catalogues sent out by many seedsmen cost twenty cents each. We thus save eighteen cents on each catalogue, and can afford to offer our seeds for less money.

We sell nothing but the best, warranted seeds. If they fail to grow, or produce true to name, through any fault of the seed, we will replace them free of charge.

Our Terms:

Cash with the order. Postage stamps taken in small quantities. Money is best sent by money order or express order.

We pay the postage on all packets, ozs., ¼lbs., and ½ pints. If you order them sent by express, you can deduct one cent from the price of an ounce, two cents from the price of ¼ lb., and four cents from the price of ½ pint. If you want pounds sent by mail, add for postage eight cents. For quarts sent by mail add sixteen cents.

If your package of seeds is lost or destroyed in the mail, we will replace it.

BEATIFUL 〰 〰 PANSIES.

N^O class of plants receives as much attention from us as pansies. They are a universally conceded favorite. We have made them our favorites. Small-flowering, poor varieties have been supplanted by large-flowering ones of the most striking colors, until we number varieties by the hundreds. No sooner does the winter snow disappear than their lovely faces appear and beautify the earth with a gorgeous festival of bloom until the mantle of snow again enshrouds them from view until the opening of another year

		Price per Pk'g
482	**Meteor**, Handsome and bright	8
483	**Claret.** Beautiful red...........	8
484	**King of Blacks.** Deep coal black	5
485	**White.** Very white strain...........................	5
486	**Pure Yellow.** Large golden yellow..................	5
487	**Dark Purple.** Deep rich color, very handsome	5
488	**Bronze.** Beautiful bronze color.....................	5
489	**Mahogany Color.** Very rich and handsome..........	5
490	**Havana Brown.** Extremely showy..................	5
491	**Silver-Edged.** Dark purple with silvery-white border	5
492	**Gold and Bronze.** Dark, beautiful gold and bronze...	5
493	**Mrs. Harrison.** Beautiful bronze color, rose margin.	5
494	**Angel of Beauty.** Pure snowy white, without eye....	6
495	**Fire Dragon.** Fiery orange and bronze with purple eye	5
496	**Rose Marbled.** Very beautiful......................	6
497	**Delicata.** Light porcelain blue with white center.....	5
498	**Odier of Blotched.** Flowers have a superb, large eye, and are beautifully blotched with rich varied colors	10
499	**Prince Bismark.** Brown and golden bronze marbled.	5
500	**Lord Baconsfield.** Large flowers of deep purple violet, top petals shaded to light blue, most effective.......	5
501	**Pelargoniflora.** Resembles the large fancy Geraniums	5
502	**Emperor William.** A well-defined purple violet eye, with main ground of ultramarine blue.............	5
503	**Stained and Striped.** Stripings and markings very fine	5
504	**Quadricolor.** Upper petal violet, sky-blue margin; lower purple on light ground; blue marbled and spotted	5
505	**Lady in White or Snow Flake.** Pure white, no eye.	5
506	**French Faced.** Mixed distinct faced varieties, largely in blue and purple shades, very large and handsome.	6
507	**Giant Trimardeau.** Colossal in size; runs through a mixture of colors, wonderfully improved in form.....	10
508	**Cassier's Giant Odier** Flowers of good substance, fine form and neat growth, immense size, three or five spotted on rich back ground of bright colors..:.....	10
509	**Bell's Ever-Blooming Greenland.** Choice strain in mixture...................................	8
510	**Bell's English Show.** Large, well-defined blossoms, plants compact and very free blooming............	8
511	**Fine Mixture.** (1/4 oz 25 cts.)......................	5
512	**Bugnot's Large Flowering.** Extra fine and large....	10
737	**Butterfly Pansy.** Very beautiful class, much advertised, flowers fine substance and rich colors	

☞ *One package each of the above 32 varieties, only $1.50; catalogue price, $2.01.*

SHOWY POPPIES.

514	New "Shirley" Poppy. Is perfectly hardy, and flowers profusely the first season from the seed. The flowers are large, graceful and elegant; colors pure, soft and varied, ranging from blush white, rose, delicate pink and carmine through innumerable tints to bright crimson. A lovely flower......... 4
515	Double Carnation Flowered. Blossoms round and double; finely fringed; remain long time in bloom 8
516	Mikado. One of the most charming double striped poppies. Petals at edge cut and fringed, and of a brilliant crimson scarlet, while the base of the petal is of a pure white. ·..................... 4
517	Peacock Poppy. Brilliant scarlet, with conspicuous glossy black ring surrounding crimson center. 4
518	Iceland Poppies. Hardy perennials, but flower the first year from seed. Elegant, satin-like flowers, very fragrant; blossoms profusely produced throughout summer and autumn; lasts long when cut 4
519	Danebrog. Brilliant scarlet with large white spots 8

BEAUTIFUL, FRAGRANT, SWEET PEAS

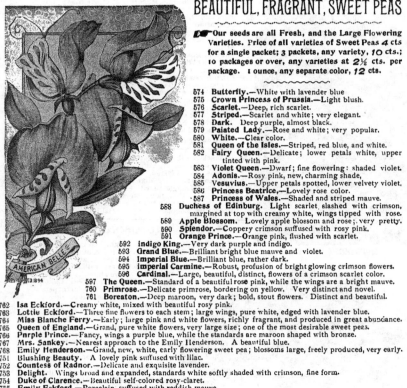

☞ **Our seeds are all Fresh, and the Large Flowering Varieties. Price of all varieties of Sweet Peas 4 cts for a single packet; 3 packets, any variety, 10 cts.; 10 packages or over, any varieties at 2½ cts. per package. 1 ounce, any separate color, 12 cts.**

574 **Butterfly.**—White with lavender blue
575 **Crown Princess of Prussia.**—Light blush.
576 **Scarlet.**—Deep, rich scarlet.
577 **Striped.**—Scarlet and white; very elegant.
578 **Dark.** Deep purple, almost black.
579 **Painted Lady.**—Rose and white; very popular.
580 **White.**—Clear color.
581 **Queen of the Isles.**—Striped, red blue, and white.
582 **Fairy Queen.**—Delicate; lower petals white, upper tinted with pink.
583 **Violet Queen.**—Dwarf; fine flowering; shaded violet.
584 **Adonis.**—Rosy pink, new, charming shade.
585 **Vesuvius.**—Upper petals spotted, lower velvety violet.
586 **Princess Beatrice,**—Lovely rose color.
587 **Princess of Wales.**—Shaded and striped mauve.
588 **Duchess of Edinburg.** Light scarlet slashed with crimson, margined at top with creamy white, wings tipped with rose.
589 **Apple Blossom.** Lovely apple blossom and rose; very pretty.
590 **Splendor.**—Coppery crimson suffused with rosy pink.
591 **Orange Prince.**—Orange pink, flushed with scarlet.
592 **indigo King.**—Very dark purple and indigo.
593 **Grand Blue.**—Brilliant bright blue mauve and violet.
594 **imperial Blue.**—Brilliant blue, rather dark.
595 **imperial Carmine.**—Robust, profusion of bright glowing crimson flowers.
596 **Cardinal.**—Large, beautiful, distinct, flowers of a crimson scarlet color.
597 **The Queen.**—Standard of a beautiful rose pink, while the wings are a bright mauve.
760 **Primrose.**—Delicate primrose, bordering on yellow. Very distinct and novel.
761 **Boreaton.**—Deep maroon, very dark; bold, stout flowers. Distinct and beautiful.
762 **Isa Eckford.**—Creamy white, mixed with beautiful rosy pink.
763 **Lottie Eckford.**—Three fine flowers to each stem; large wings, pure white, edged with lavender blue.
764 **Miss Blanche Ferry.**—Early; large pink and white flowers, richly fragrant, and produced in great abundance.
765 **Queen of England.**—Grand, pure white flowers, very large size; one of the most desirable sweet peas.
766 **Purple Prince.**—Fancy, wings a purple blue, while the standards are maroon shaped with bronze.
767 **Mrs. Sankey.**—Nearest approach to the Emily Henderson. A beautiful blue.
768 **Emily Henderson.**—Grand, new, white, early flowering sweet pea; blossoms large, freely produced, very early.
751 **Blushing Beauty.** A lovely pink suffused with lilac.
752 **Countess of Radnor.**—Delicate and exquisite lavender.
753 **Delight.** Wings broad and expanded, standards white softly shaded with crimson, fine form.
754 **Duke of Clarence.**—Beautiful self-colored rosy-claret.
755 **Emily Eckford.**—Porcelain, suffused with reddish mauve.
756 **Empress of India.**—Grand, rosy pink standards, white wings.
757 **Lemon Queen.** Grand large flower of delicate blush with wings faintly tinted lemon.
758 **Mrs. Eckford.**—Best yellow shades being a combination of beautiful primrose and sulphur yellow, large, fine.
759 **Miss Hunt**—Charming carmine-salmon and soft pink combined.
769 **Mrs. Gladstone.**—Blossoms of perfect form, color of the most delicate pink with rosy blush wings.
770 **Monarch.** Magnificent flowers, with a rich deep blue, and standards of bronzy-crimson or dark maroon.
771 **Princess Louise.**—Rich, rosy-pink standards with wings of lilac blue.
772 **Rose and White.**— Pretty combinations of the two colors.
773 **Senator.**—Standards striped chocolate brown purple on creamy white ground, wings a deep purple striped.
598 **Beautiful Home Mixture.**—Saved only from our choice strains, and Eckford's new sorts. Oz. 20 cts.; ¼ lb. 40c.
600 **Fancy Mixed.**—The above and many other choice sorts. This mixture is much superior to that usually sold. Oz. 10 cts.; ¼ lb. 20 cts.; 1 lb. 40 cts.

EVERLASTING OR PERENNIAL PEA.

802 **Lathyrus, Splendens.** One of the finest flowers offered. It bears great, dense clusters of brilliant deep rose flowers. Known in the West as "Pride of California. Price per packet 8
803 **Everlasting Pea.** Perennial, dies down to ground, and starts every spring.. 6
804 **Lathyrus, Rotundifolius.** Hardy; small, oval leaves make a pleasing background for the bright rosy flowers; blooms much earlier than the annual sweet peas. 6
774 **Trailing Lord Anson Pea.**—Bushy and trailing, with large flowers of the richest colors; commences to bloom sooner than the sweet peas. Mixed colors. Price per package 5
Double White Hardy Pea. Very beautiful and popular 6

DOUBLE SWEET PEAS.

These grand novelties will this season be the most sought for of any flowers. Everyone must have them or be behind the times. Our assortment includes all the double varieties in fine mixed colors. Price per large package, 10 cents; three packages, 25 cents.

GRAND NEW, WHITE, EARLY-FLOWERING SWEET PEA, "BLANCHE BURPEE."
Blossoms large, clear and freely produced; blooms two weeks earlier than most varieties. Per package, 8c., 4 pk'g 25c

SNOWDRIFT POPPY.

520	**Riverdale Mixture.** Hundreds of choice showy varieties; best mixture ever offered....[¼oz. 10?]....	8
521	**Mephisto.** Lovely scarlet, with blackish purple spots	4
522	**Umbrosum.** Showy; vermillion studded with jet spots	4
523	**Double Pompone.** Dwarf, double flowers varied colors	4
524	**Spotted Beauty.** Deep red scarlet spotted with white	4
525	**Striped Beauty.** Pure white ground, dark red stripes	5
526	**Chamois Rose.** New colors, large, ball-shaped flowers	4
527	**New Oriental.** A new hybrid, containing a charming variety of new varied colors; extremely beautiful	4
529	**Fairy Blush Poppy.** The finest of all; immense globular flowers, 10 to 13 in. in circumference; fringed petals, pure white with rosy cream tips; foliage 10 to 14 in. high, above which appear the flowers.....	5
530	**Snowdrift.** Pure snowy white, very double, large size, neat and compact; very desirable...........	5
531	**The Bride.** New single white; satiny finish; can be preserved long time in water; valuable cut flower	5

One package each of 20 varieties of Poppies, 60 cts.

543	**Pysanthus Albens.** Rapid climber; white flowers; traps insects...................	4
544	**Picotee,** Finest Mixed. Lovely fragrant plant........	10
545	**Platycodons,** Fancy Mixed. Very showy and grand	4
546	**Portulacca,** Single Mixed. Showy trailing plant, dazzling rich flowers, adapted for vases....	3
546½	" Double Mixed. Full and double as roses	8
547	**Potentilla,** Double. Fine perennial, beautiful flowers	5

PHLOX DRUMMONDII.

549	**Cuspidata, Star of Quedlinburgh.** The most unique of all Phloxes; the long, pointed central teeth of the petals form a complete star; variety of colors.	10
550	**Scarlet.** Very brilliant.........	5
551	**Alba.** Pure white.............	5
563	**Frimbriata or Fringed.** Closely related to the Cuspidata; petals sometimes not cut or fringed	8
552	**Variabilis.** Violet and lilac.....	5
553	**Rosea.** Rose, white eyes.....	5
554	**Grandiflora.** Largest flower...	6
555	**Dwarf Mammoth.** Plants dwarf, flowers large; all desirable col's	10
556	**New Double White.** Free flowering, large blossoms, double...	10
557	**Black Warrior.** Deep blood red.	6
558	**Meteor.** Fiery scarlet, very dazzling, one of the most brilliant	6
559	**Pale Yellow.** Novel, excellent..	6
560	**Stellata.** Very dazzling with a white center, blooms freely...	3
561	**Verbena Flowered.** Novel and showy, not ordinary	6
562	**The Palisade Mixture.** A mixture of all rare sorts	8
564	**Fine Mixed.** All varieties........[¼ oz. 20c.]....	4

One package of each of the 16 varieties of Phlox, 80 cts.

DOUBLE PORTULACCA.

PRIMULA, or Chinese Primrose.

565	**Choice Fringed.** Beautifully cut flowers, mixed colors......................[15 seeds]....	10
566	**Fimbriata.** Pure white, semi-double, [12 seeds]...	10
567	**Double Mixed.** Very choice..........[10 seeds].	25
568	**Double White.** Finely fringed...... [10 seeds].	25
569	**Double Striped.** Fancy, beautifully striped [10]	25
570	**Rosea.** Free growing, 10 or 12 spikes cored with rosy carmine flowers, yellow eye, hardy, [25 "]	15
571	**Obsconica.** New; pale lilac; blooms in 3 months from sowing and continues all winter [15 seeds]	10
572	**Floribunda.** One of the prettiest: rich green leaves, red stems, yellow flowers; vigorous grower.....	15

Phlox, Star of Quedlinburgh   **Phlox Fimbriata.**

704	**PRIMULA JAPONICA.** (Japanese Primrose.) Showy flowers in whirls on long stems, mixed colors..	10

573	**Polyanthus Primula.** Mixed. Very hardy and pretty border plant for early spring flowering	5
605	**Pyrethrum,** Golden Feather. Very desirable for borders; bright yellow foliage............	5
606	" White Bouquet. Fancy double white variety, good for cut flowers	3
607	" Large Flowered Single. Very fine for permanent beds; showy colors	5
608	" Cinerariefolium. The variety that is grown for Dalmatian Insect Powder............	5
609	" Roseum. The "Persian Insect Powder Plant." Destroys insects on plants near it; rose-colored blossoms.	8

Gather blossoms when fully open, dry thoroughly; powder before using; mix with ten parts flour.

LIST of NEW AND STANDARD VEGETABLE SEEDS

We have here listed everything which we consider best adapted for all climates. We believe we offer just as good sorts, if not better, than any we omit. New varieties are added as soon as their value is determined. Many new varieties are worthless, but are put on the market at a high price with a lavish description with no other possible object than to delude the public and give the seller a big profit.

WE OFFER Nothing but the Best. All our seeds are grown with great care, and can be relied upon to be *fresh, true to name*, and of the *highest quality*. No one can sell you better seeds, even if they do publish a gaudy catalogue of 100 to 200 pages, filled with lavish descriptions, telling what superior seeds they have. We could name half a dozen seedsmen who tell what superior seeds they offer, and charge exorbitant prices for the same, who buy the cheapest possible stock they can get in the south and west, and try to palm it off for northern grown.

NO DISCOUNT ON THESE PRICES.

Packages of Beans, Peas or Corn are 4 cents each by mail or 3 cents if sent by express.

The price in the first column is for one half pint of seed by mail post-paid. If you want the half pint sent by express, deduct 4 cents from this price. Quarts, Pecks and Bushels are by express, purchaser paying express charges. If you want a Quart sent by mail, add 15 cents to the price named to pay postage. Customers living at a distance who only want a few quarts, will find it cheaper to add the 15 cents and have them sent by mail.

BUSH OR DWARF BEANS.—(Green Podded Varieties.)

	½ pt.	Qt.	Peck	Bush.
Early Red Valentine, a good, extra early variety. Crisp and fine quality............	10¢	15¢	95¢	$3 25
Early White Valentine, differ from the preceeding only in color. Very fine.........	10	18	1 10	3 75
Early Mohawk, very early and productive. Best early variety	10	18	95	3 45
Best of All, fleshy, succulent, stringless, extra green podded variety; great bearer...	10	18	1 10	3 75
Early Refugee, very early and great bearer..........................	10	18	1 00	3 75
Horticultural Dwarf, very popular; called cranberry; best for green shelled	10	18	1 00	3 75
Prolific Tree, Improved, great cropper, small white, good for field crop.............	10	15	95	3 50
White Marrow, best white for field crop. Of good size and productive.............	10	15	95	3 45
Henderson's Bush Lima, earliest bush lima. Earlier than pole limas...............	14	25	1 50	5 40
Burpee's Bush Lima, the largest and best of the bush limas....................	15	35	2 00	7 50
Dreer's Bush Lima, a well-recommended variety ....;........	15	40	2 50	9 00

BUSH BEANS, YELLOW PODDED OR WAX.

	½ pt.	Qt.	Peck	Bush.
Saddleback Wax, pods large, long, straight, round and full of meat; absolutely string less, vigorous grower, profuse bearer, plants average 30 to 40 pods on each, filled with solid pulp between the beans.........................	18	45	2 75	9 50
Ivory Pod Wax, early, almost transparent, long and stringless, waxy white.........	12	22	1 25	4 45
Early Golden Wax, excellent, early stringless variety, one of the best for family use	10	18	1 20	3 25
Date Wax, prolific handsome variety, early, keeps stringless a long time............	10	20	1 45	4 50
Kidney Wax, largest and handsomest early bush bean, productive and fine quality..	12	24	1 40	4 75
Yosemite Mammoth Wax, pods often 10 to 12 inches long; fine quality, all solid pulp, cooks tender and delicious, one bush will produce 50 pods..................	18	35	1 95	7 50
Ferry's Detroit Wax, handsome, productive, fine shelled	12	22	1 50	4 90
Prolific German Black Wax, strong robust grower, productive, tender, excellent quality	12	22	1 45	4 80
German White Wax, fine quality, extra white wax variety, productive, desirable....	14	25	1 45	5 00
Long Yellow Six Weeks, very early and withall an extra garden variety..........	10	18	1 10	3 75
Currie's Rust Proof Wax, early, upright grower, robust, productive, does not rust...	12	24	1 50	5 00

POLE OR CLIMBING BEANS.

	½ pt.	Qt.	Peck	Bush.
Old Homestead, early and best green-podded variety; stringless, tender and melting; cooks well; pods filled with enormous clusters, enormously productive.........	15	35	2 00	7 50
Horticultural or Cranberry, a hardy, productive and prized variety, good to shell...	12	25	1 65	5 75
Dutch Case Knife, an old standard green-podded variety, productive and early......	10	20	1 45	5 00
Lazy Wife, an enormous yielder, green pod, luscious and tender ....:	15	30	2 00	7 50
Golden Champion, extra early, large size, light yellow pod, absolutely stringless, cooks tender and luscious, very productive, does not rust easily.....................	18	35	2 25	7 75
Golden Wax Flageolet, vine crowded with long yellow pods, early, excellent quality	15	25	1 85	6 75
Golden Andalusia Wax. This is the most wonderful pole bean ever offered. One-half bushel of beautiful golden pods are often taken from one vine at a picking. Pods large, broad, fleshy, entirely stringless and unsurpassed in flavor. Begins to bear while very young and continues throughout entire season	20	40	3 00	9 50
Golden Cluster Wax, early, yellow pods, grows in clusters, prolific, extra quality, poles ten feet high often crowded with beautiful luscious pods, good shelled....	15	35	1 95	6 85
Early Jersey Lima, the earliest of pole limas with large beans	12	30	1 85	6 L0
King of the Garden Limas, large, vigorous, productive; best of the large late limas...	14	30	1 90	6 75

PEAS:

☞ All Best Northern Grown and Hand-picked.

	½ pt.	Qt.	Peck	Bush.
Bell's Extra Early, an extra early variety, two to two and a half ft. high, productive	10	15	90	3 50
American Wonder, extra early dwarf, 6 inches high, fine quality................	10	18	1 10	4 25
Alaska, well known, extra early, blue pea, two feet high, productive,..............	10	16	95	4 00
McLean's Advancer, fine market garden variety, early, productive, good quality....	10	15	95	3 45
Blue Beauty, nearly two feet high, uniform, productive, round blue..................	10	18	1 00	3 75
Horsford's Market Garden, best for market garden, early, productive, sweet, bushy..	10	15	95	3 50
Premium Gem, dwarf, with large well filled pods, early wrinkled variety..........	10	15	95	3 40
Bliss' Everbearing, of strong, stocky growth, producing a great crop of large, sweet, wrinkled peas; continuous bearer, vines have had 100 pods at a time..........	12	20	1 00	3 75
Bliss' Abundance, 18 inches high, medium early, pods filled with luscious, green, wrinkled peas. Productive, branches like a tree, bears continuously..........	12	20	1 00	3 75
Burpee's Quality, of excellent quality and yields well,.........................	12	20	1 10	4 25

NEW GOLDEN ANDALUSIA BEAN

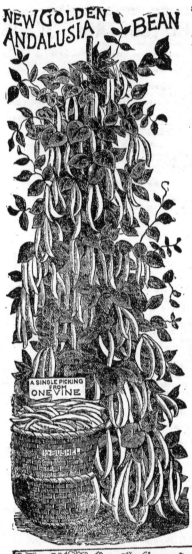

A SINGLE PICKING FROM ONE VINE

½ BUSHEL

Packages of Beans, Peas or Corn 4 cents each by mail or 3 cents each by express. Half pints by mail at prices quoted. Quarts or over are quoted by express, purchaser paying charges; if wanted by mail, add 15 cents per quart.

KIDNEY WAX BEAN.

Half pint, 15¢ ; 1 quart, 24¢ ; 1 peck, $1.40; 1 bushel, $4.75.

GOLDEN WAX BEAN.

½ pint, 10¢ ; 1 qt., 18¢ ; 1 peck, $1.20; 1 bushel, $3.25.

LATWIFE'S POLE BEAN

Early Golden Cluster Wax Bean.

The Corn we grow for seed.

PEAS—continued

	½pt.	Qt.	peck	bush.
Mammoth Edible-Pod Sugar, good cooked pods and all, same as string beans,	13¢	?.	$1 75	$6 00
Telephone, immensely productive, a grand, large, sweet pea, vines tall	12	20	1 10	4 25
Champion of England, the old standard, tall, medium late, great bearer, good seller.	10	14	85	2 90
Large White Marrowfat, an old standard and great bearer for late crop	9	12	65	1 95
Black-Eyed Marrowfat, grown largely by sowing with oats, etc., for late	9	12	65	1 95

SWEET OR SUGAR CORN.

Early Cory, the earliest grown; fair sized ears, comes into the market two weeks ahead of most early varieties; exquisitely sweet flavor	10	15	75	2 75
Early White Cory, resembles the Early Cory in size and earliness, but is pure white	10	18	90	3 25
Livingston's Gold Coin, a grand yielder, very rich, yellow color	10	15	95	3 90
Bell's Mammoth Sugar, mammoth ears, coming into market ahead of Stowell's Evergreen, fine quality, pronounced by many to be superior to the Evergreen	10	15	75	2 50
Shakers' Early, early, large ears, pearly white, productive, vigorous, sweet	10	15	80	2 75
Early Minnesota, an old standard early variety; very desirable, good size	10	15	80	2 75
Early Maine, profitable for market growers, pure white cob, kernels sweet and juicy	10	15	80	2 75
Burlington Hybrid, very large ears, extra early for size, unusually productive	10	18	90	3 00
Perry's Hybrid, large, early, sweet, best 2nd early, maturing after Cory. large kernel	10	15	80	2 75
Red-Cob Evergreen, earlier than Stowell's and a good bearer	10	18	95	3 40
Country Gentleman, resembles the old Shoepeg, good size, long kernel, swee', tender	10	18	90	3 00
Stowell's Evergreen, the old standard late variety, mammoth ears, fine quality	10	15	70	2 50

FIELD CORN.

King of the Earlies, an extra early, good field variety, for extreme north	10	15	70	1 75
Longfellow, eight-rowed, yellow flint, cob small, extra northern variety	10	15	70	1 75
Golden Beauty Dent, perfect shape, 10 to 16 rows, large size, not ripen too far north.	10	15	70	1 75
Champion White Pearl Dent, pure white, early for dent, very prolific, best every way	10	15	70	1 75
POP CORN, White Rice, best all-round variety of Pop Corn in cultivation	10	25	1 50	4 75

MISCELLANEOUS SEEDS.

Packages, ounces and one-fourth pounds mailed free at prices given. Pounds are by express. If pounds are wanted by mail add eight cents postage for each pound. Where the price per ounce is 20 cents or over, one-half ounce will be supplied at half the price of an ounce.

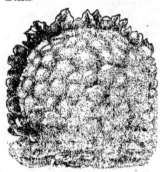

Henderson's Early Snowball CAULIFLOWER.

	Pkt.	Oz.	¼lb.	lb.
ASPARAGUS, Palmetto, mammoth size, extra quality, has no superior	4¢	12¢	35¢	95
ASPARAGUS, Conover's Collossal, old standard variety, hardy, good large grower,	3	7	14	30
ASPARAGUS, California Mammoth White, new, very large, superior white variety,	5	20	65	$1 50
BORECOLE, or KALE, Green Curled standard s rt, bright green hardy.	3	8	25	65
BRUSSELS SPROUTS, delicious vegetable with numerous little heads resembling small cabbages,	3	10	30	95
CRESS, or PEPPERGRASS, Fine Curled, a very superior variety of this popular salad,	3	7	15	38
COLLARDS, Georgia, popular in the south, open heads,	3	9	20	60
CAULIFLOWER, Early London, well known and much grown, early sort	3	35	$1 20	$4 50
CAULIFLOWER, Extra Early Dwarf Erfurt's, largely grown, sure header	8	1 50	5 75	22 00
CAULIFLOWER, Henderson's Early Snowball, best all round sort, sure header, well known, fine quality... (¼ oz. 50c. ; one tenth oz. 25c)	10	1 75	6 25	23 50
CAULIFLOWER, Bell's Early Surehead, called where grown the best and surest bearing cauliflower; good size, fine quality, extra early. (one-tenth oz 35c.; ¼oz. 75c.; ½oz. $1.40)	10	2 80	9 00	35 00
CHICCORY, Large-Rooted or Coffee, used as a substitute for coffee,	3	9	20	70
CORN SALAD, used much the same as spinach,	3	15	50	1 75
EGG PLANT, Early Long Purple, early, good cropper, easy to cultivate,	3	15	50	1 90
" " New York Improved, most popular sort, large, fine quality (½ oz. 13c.)	4	25	85	3 25
KOHL RABI, Early White Vienna, best for table or market,	4	14	40	1 25
MUSHROOM SPAWN, comes in bricks, 1 lb 30c.; 2 lbs. 45c. by mail				
MUSTARD, White, best for salads or culinary purposes,	2	6	14	30
" Black or Brown, stronger than the white	2	7	15	33
OKRA, White Velvet, finest quality, not prickly,	3	9	25	75
PARSLEY, Giant Curled, large, finely curled, popular,	3	8	20	50
" Fern-Leaved, ornamental and fine	3	8	22	60
RHUBARB, Large Victoria, mammoth size, good quality, late	3	12	45	1 25
" Linnaeus good size, tender, early,	3	12	45	1 25
SALSIFY or VEGETABLE OYSTER, White French, used as a substitute for oysters	3	10	30	40
" " " Mammoth Sandwich Island, large smooth white,	4	15	45	1 25
SPINACH, Round or Summer, best early for spring sowing	2	6	14	25
" Prickley of Fall, hardy, to sow in fall	2	6	14	25
" Bloomsdale Savoy Leaved, pretty good quality	3	7	15	28
" Long Standing, one of the best market varieties, thick green leaves	3	6	14	25

Vine Peach

This fruit is some larger than a large peach, of a bright orange color when ripe. For sweet pickles, sauce, pies, or preserving it is superb. Easily cultivated, same as melon or cucumber; wonderfully productive, used same as a peach only not so good to eat uncooked...... Pkt. 5c.; 1 oz. 25c ¼lb. 80c.; 1 lb. $2.50.

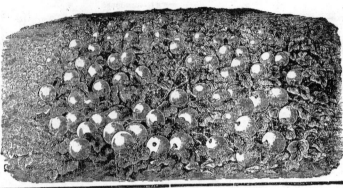

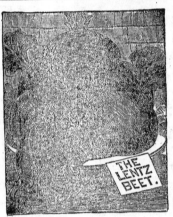

THE LENTZ BEET.

Long Blood Red, popular winter variety, fine quality, good yielder ·············

BEETS, (Table Varieties.)

	Pkt.	Oz.	¼lb.	lb.
Eclipse, round, dark red, extra early, very sweet, look fine and sell well......	3¢	8¢	15¢	$ 38
Egyptian Turnip, popular only for early bunching, dark red and no seller,...	3	8	15	38
Lentz's Extra Early Blood Turnip, deep color, better than Egyptian in every way and fully as early....................	3	8	17	40
Mitchell's Perfected Turnip, earliest of any, perfect shape, deep color, small top, the b st for general planting by market gardeners....................	3	9	18	45
Edmand's Early Turnip, uniform, handsome, small top. fine appearance, second early, deep red....................	3	7	15	35
Early Bassano, popular variety with many well known, good quality, flat.........	3	7	15	35
Dewing's Improved Blood Turnip, called an improvement on the old Blood Turnip	3	8	16	38
Blood Turnip, the old standard variety so extensively grown, dark red...........	3	7	15	35
Bastain's Blood Turnip, fine for second early crop, similar to Blood Turnip, crisp	3	7	15	35
Imperial Sugar, grown for table and stock An immense cropper, ...	3	7	14	30
White French Sugar, great yielder and profitable for stock or sale.............	3	7	14	30
	3	7	15	35

MANGLE WURTZEL BEETS. (For Stock.)

	Pkt.	Oz.	¼lb.	lb.
Golden Tankard, nutritious, great milk producer, yields 50 to 75 tons per acre	3	7	14	25
Prize Long Red, large size, good quality, immensely productive, improved red............	3	6	12	25
Improved Yellow Globe, best of all the round varieties; keeps well ·················	3	7	14	25
Bon's Giant of the Plains, grows half above the ground and of tremendous size. ········	3	8	15	30

CARROTS.

Oxheart or Guerande Carrot.

	Pkt.	Oz.	¼lb.	lb.
Early French Forcing, extra early, small variety, fine quality,....................	3	8	20	65
Danvers Half Long, dark orange, productive, handsome, uniform, half long,...........	3	8	20	60
Oxheart or Guerande, extra table variety, grows good size, with short roots..............	3	8	22	70
Intermediate Scarlet, rich orange red, long, productive....................	3	7	15	65
Half Long Stump-Rooted, great yielder........	3	7	15	65
Improved Long Orange, standard variety, long, well-formed roots, good keeper, deep orange.	3	7	15	45
Long White Belgian, white, grown mostly for stock, immense yielder......................	3	7	15	40

CABBAGES.

We sell nothing but the best stock, and nearly all our seed is grown by the best growers on Long Island. We offer none but what the most critical market gardeners can depend upon as being the best possible to obtain,

	Pkt.	Oz.	¼lb.	lb.
Early York, popular small heading variety,....................	3	10	35	$1 00

CABBAGES.—continued.

Early Winningstadt.

Bell's Mammoth Wakefield.

	Pkt.	Oz.	¼lb.	lb.
Early Winningstadt, best for general gardens for early or late, heads hard, pointed, sure to head up.......	3¢	10¢	35¢	$1 00
Early French Oxheart, a fair early variety,..........	3	10	35	1 00
Early Jersey Wakefield, extensively grown for early market, compact grower, very early, fine quality..	4	15	50	1 50
Bell's Mammoth Wakefield, resembles the Wakefield, but much larger and a few days later,............	4	18	60	1 75
Early Etampes, small, compact, extra early, fine flavor	4	12	45	1 35
Henderson's Early Summer, one of the very best for second early, solid, good size and fine quality.....	4	12	45	1 45
Fottler's Improved Brunswick, a well known good sized second early, ...	4	12	40	1 30
Nonesuch, extra fine quality, good grower and keeper.	4	12	50	1 45
Premium Flat Dutch, the best old standard variety, grown more than any other. Our stock is extra fine, selected from best heads. We have an extra large stock and offer it low. Sure to do well	3	10	35	1 00
Warren Stone Mason, becoming very popular; extra solid, small head, best shipper grown,..........................	4	15	45	1 50
All Seasons or Vandegaw, heads large, round and flattened at top, second early	4	14	40	1 35
Henderson's Succession, medium early, solid, large; whole fields head up without showing hardly a poor bead	4	14	40	1 35
Large Late Drumhead, large heads popular	4	10	35	1 10
All Head, a medium early, extra solid, all head, (no waste or poor heads) excellent keeper, fine quality, tender, good, and profitable for market................	4	15	45	1 45
Mammoth Red Rock, the largest and best of all the red cabbages	4	20	60	1 75
Bell's Improved Excelsior Flat Dutch, sure header, large, solid keeper, fine market	4	20	60	1 75
Marblehead Mammoth, the largest cabbage grown, a reliable header	4	15	45	1 50
Drumhead Savoy, the best of the Savoys, extra quality, good keeper, ...	4	15	45	1 45
Bell's Surehead, every plant produces a solid head, fine flavor, good for home use or shipping, very solid and heavy with few outer leaves	4	15	50	1 50
Autumn King or World Beater, the finest large, late, dark green cabbage, reliable header with few outer leaves, keeps longer than almost any other sort; try it for late....	4	15	50	1 50

FLAT DUTCH.

BELL'S SUREHEAD.

CUCUMBER.

	Pkt.	Oz.	¼lb.	lb.
Early Cluster, productive, grows in clusters, very early.................................	3	7	15	40
Early Frame, or Short Green, good extra early variety, well formed...................	3	7	15	40
Early Russian, very early, crisp, tender and popular; grows in clusters	3	7	15	45
Chicago Pickling, productive and very desirable for pickling, good for market..........	3	7	15	45
Giant Pera, very large, 18 to 20 inches long, prolific and tender........................	3	8	18	50
White Spine, productive, long, full at end, popular, good market variety,.............	3	7	15	45
Improved Long Green, standard variety, long, best for table and general crop,..........	3	7	15	40
New Everbearing, everbearing in character commences to bear extra early and continues until frosts, whether ripe fruit is picked or not; solid and fine quality..............	4	10	25	65
White Pearl, fruit white from the first, very hardy and produces a large crop, uniform..	4	12	28	75
White Wonder, white, handsome, fine quality, very hardy and a strong grower, will do well where many of the delicate sorts fail; uniform color, shape and size, about eight inches long, skin thin, pearly white, flesh brittle and exquisitely fine, sure cropper,..	5	15	35	95

Bell's Prolific Pickling Cucumber.

Undoubtedly one of the best varieties for pickling. Good size, uniform shape superior quality, immensely productive.

Pkt.........	4¢
Oz	10
¼ lb	25
lb	70

Improved Golden Self-Blanching.

CELERY.

	Pkt,	Oz	¼lb.	lb.
Golden-Hearted Dwarf, solid, fine flavor, good keeper,..................	3¢	15¢	40¢	$1 30
Rose, ornamental, fine flavor, fine keeper	3	12	35	1 25
Improved Golden Self-Blanching, best for general cultivation; perfect keeper, blanches without banking up, ribs light yellow, heart golden yellow crisp, solid, and the best possible flavor, ribs thick and closely set ...... (½ ounce, 15 cents.)	4	30	95	3 00
Kalamazoo, perfect type of dwarf with broad ribs, handsome, crisp, good keeper, creamy white color,................	4	20	60	2 00
Giant Pascal, large, broad, thick and crisp; excellent keeper, fine nutty flavor, blanches easily in 5 or 6 days, full heart and broad heavy ribs	4	15	50	1 75
Improved White Plume, popular self-blanching, will whiten by tying up leaves and hoeing up a little earth, early, crisp and good flavor,..................	4	15	50	1 75
Celeriac, or Turnip-rooted Celery, grown for the large, turnip-shaped roots, which make excellent salad cooked or sliced in vinegar; tender and rich and fine for seasoning meat or flavoring soups	3	12	40	1 25

LETTUCE.

Ferry's Early Prize-Head.

Hanson.

Golden Ball, very popular and good flavor, fine for home use. Pkt, 3¢; oz., 8¢; ¼lb., 22¢; pound. 75¢

Silver Ball, pretty, solid heads tender, good, keeps well. Pkt, 3¢; oz., 9¢; ¼lb., 22¢; pound. 75¢

Butter Cup, rich buttery sort, crisp and tender, keeps well. Pkt. 3¢; oz., 8¢; ¼lb., 22¢; pound, 75¢.

	Pkt.	Oz.	¼lb.	lb.
Early Tennis Ball, early variety with small. solid head, hardy	2¢	8¢	22¢	75
Tomhannock, large, beautiful upright, white, crisp, tender, grows quickly	3	8	20	65
Salamander, good size, compact, stands heat and drouth well, slow going to seed..........	3	8	20	60

LETTUCE.—Continued.

	Pkt.	Oz.	¼lb.	lb.
Marblehead Mammoth, large size, resembles a cabbage, early, tender, good, crisp	3	9	22	$ 65
Hanson, great favorite, large, excellent quality, grows quickly, stands summer well	3	9	20	65
Ferry's Early Prize-Head, large plants, fine curled, crisp, fine flavor, lasts well	3	9	20	65
California All-Heart, extra fine lettuce, handsome pointed head, rich, buttery, solid	3	10	25	90
Defiance, large heads, always fine quality, solid and slow to go to seed	3	10	25	75
Big Boston, large and solid, good for forcing, or out doors	3	10	22	70
Grand Rapids, excellent for forcing, grows quickly and tender, fine shipper	3	10	22	70
Denver Market, delicate, handsome, tender, excellent quality, resembles Savoy cabbage	3	10	22	75

WATERMELON.

	Pkt.	Oz.	¼lb.	lb.
Dixie, large, handsome, fine quality, thin rind, uniform size, good shipper	3	9	15	45
Mountain Sweet, early, oblong in shape, sweet and rich, hardy	3	7	14	40
Cuban Queen, a large, solid, shipping melon, often weighs 100 pounds, great favorite	3	7	15	40
Ice Cream, or Peerless, extra fine, solid, sweet, thin rind, good for general crop	3	7	15	40
Kolb Gem, the great shipper, prolific, large, hardy and beautiful, largely grown	3	7	15	40
Hungarian Honey, honey sweet, bright red, melting, luscious and early	3	10	25	70
Iron Clad, very hardy, ships well, good flavor, oblong and productive, large size	3	8	15	40
Scaly Bark, a strong, vigorous grower, producing large, solid fruit	3	7	14	40
Vick's Early, a good early melon of excellent quality, flesh pink and solid	3	7	15	45
Ruby Gold, flesh solid, golden yellow, pretty, weighs about 40 pounds each	3	8	15	45
Boss, dark skin, very solid and sweet	3	8	15	40

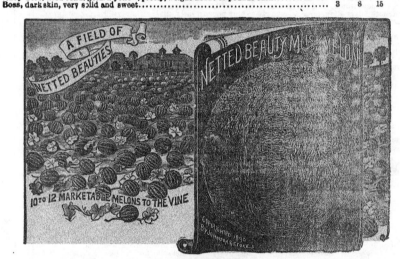

A FIELD OF NETTED BEAUTIES — 10 to 12 MARKETABLE MELONS TO THE VINE

NETTED BEAUTY MUSKMELON

MUSKMELON.

	Pkt.	Oz.	¼lb.	lb.
Netted Beauty, a new early variety, luscious flavor, vines bear from 8 to 10 melons each	4	12	35	$1 00
Jersey Belle, early and of good size, one of the best in every way	4	10	30	95
Banquet, finely netted, red flesh, very productive, unsurpassed in rich flavor	4	12	35	1 00
Shumway's Giant, mammoth size and well spoken of by market growers	3	10	30	80
New Melrose, one of the best ever introduced; prolific, unsurpassed in quality	4	12	35	1 00
Bay View, a good standard variety, strong grower, good size, fine quality	3	7	15	45
Extra Early Hackensack, a very popular sort with growers, ribbed, early, good seller	3	7	15	45
Improved Casaba, of large size, delicious flavor and a sure cropper	3	7	15	45
Montreal Market, large size, ribbed, thick and solid, of rich melting flavor	3	7	15	45
Delmonico, a variety highly prized by market growers	3	7	15	45
Early Jenny Lind, extra early, sells well at a good price	3	7	15	45
Emerald Gem, deep emerald green, thin rind, flesh suffused with salmon color	3	8	18	50
Princess, flesh thick, salmon, heavy netted, early, productive, unsurpassed in flavor	4	9	20	65
Columbus, a splendid melon either for home use or shipping	5	15	45	1 25

ONIONS.

☞ All fresh, plump seed, grown with the greatest of care.

YELLOW GLOBE DANVERS.

	Pkt.	Oz.	¼lb.	lb.
Yellow Globe Danvers. This is the standard variety for eastern markets, being more largely grown than all others combined. Well formed, good size, fine flavor, good producer and keeps well	3	10	30	90
Spanish King, mammoth size, often weighs 3 to 4 lbs. pronounced the largest, handsomest and most profitable onion grown; flesh white, sweet, mild and tender, always attracts attention in market	4	18	50	1 75
Prizetaker, resembles Spanish King but is more globe shaped, has produced over 1000 bushels to the acre	4	18	50	1 75

ONIONS—Continued.

LARGE WETHERSFIELD

	Pkt.	Oz.	¼lb.	lb.
Large Red Wethersfield, grown largely in the west, fine grained, productive, good keeper, grown in immense quantities for shipping, skin deep purplish red	3	10	35	$1 20
Extra Early Pearl, the earliest good sized white onion grown, pearly white color, mild, grows wonderfully rapid, keeps well,	4	20	65	2 25
Early White Queen, a silver-skinned variety of quick growth and good keeper, good for pickles if sown thickly, grows two inches in diameter by July	4	20	60	2 00
Bell's Rapid White Pickling, grand small early white onion for pickling, fine quality	4	20	60	2 00
Adriatic Barletta, very early, small, white, delicate, silver skin, firm, mild, fine for pickles	4	18	50	1 75
Extra Early Red, medium size, flat, red, resembles Wethersfield but two weeks earlier	3	10	35	1 20
Round Yellow Danvers, early, good for market, good size, keeps well in winter	3	10	30	90
Large Yellow Globe, or Southport, handsome, large, mild flavored, produces large crops and keeps well	4	12	35	1 10
Large Red Globe, handsome large, fine grained, mild and tender, early for size	3	10	35	1 10
Large Yellow Dutch, good size, flat, mild, keeps well, used for growing sets	3	10	30	95
Mammoth Silver King, large, weighs two to four pounds, early, silvery white, mild	4	15	50	1 75
Giant Red, or American Bermuda, mild, mammoth size, rapid grower	4	15	50	1 75
Silver Skin, large, mild, pleasant flavor, handsome silvery white, used to pickle	4	20	65	2 00
Mammoth Pompeii, enormous size, redish skin, flesh white, fine grained, mild	4	18	60	1 85
Giant Rocca, mild, delicate flavor, immense size, globe shaped	4	15	50	1 50

ONION SETS, fine quality, ½ pint, 10¢; pint, 15¢; quart, 25¢ by mail; by express, quart, 10¢; peck, 90¢; bushel, $3 25.

Perennial or Egyptian Onion Sets, very hardy, lives out during winter and produces large green tops early in spring. ½ pint, 10¢; quart, 30¢.

PEPPER.

	Pkt.	Oz.	¼lb.	lb.
Golden Upright, large size, golden yellow, productive, pleasant flavor, upright	4	20	65	2 25
Procopp's Giant, uniform, very large, 8 to 10 inches around, pleasant taste	4	20	65	2 25
Large Bell or Bull Nose, early good size, about 4 inches through, red, for stuffing	3	15	50	1 65
Long Red, productive, pungent. thick flesh, 3 to 4 inches long. (½oz. 8 cts)	3	15	50	1 75
Mammoth Golden Queen, uniform, large size, mild, delicious flavor, sells well	4	22	76	2 40
Mammoth Ruby King, plants full of large red peppers of mild, delicate flavor	4	20	65	2 00

PROCOPP'S GIANT PEPPER.

PUMPKIN.

	Pkt.	Oz.	¼lb.	lb.
King of Mammoths, large size, fine appearance often weighing 250 pounds each	4	12	35	95
Large Cheese, flat, hardy, good for cooking	3	8	15	38
Large Tours, enormous size, often weighing 320	4	12	40	60
Mammoth Potiron, large size, productive, good	4	12	40	1 00
Sugar, very sweet and solid, fine for pies	3	9	20	50
Connecticut Field, standard field sort (peck 75c)	3	6	10	25
Japanese Pie, medium size, productive, sweet as sweet potato, extra fine for pies	3	9	20	60
Golden Oblong, prolific, oblong, light yellow, fire quality	4	10	25	85
Tennessee Sweet Potato, hardy, keeps well, productive, dry, brittle, excellent flavor	3	9	25	60

☞ ½ ounces of seed quoted at 20 cents an ounce or over will be supplied at half the price of an ounce.

RADISHES .

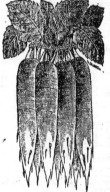

	Pkt.	Oz.	¼lb.	lb.
No Plus Ultra, an extra early new forcing variety, popular	4	10	25	75
Rose Olive-shaped, early, tender, excellent quality	3	7	16	40
Vick's Scarlet Globe, handsome globe shaped, for forcing	3	7	15	40
Early Scarlet Turnip, standard variety, best for general early crop, crisp and tender	3	7	15	35
Long Scarlet Short Top, 6 to 7 inches long, grown more than any other variety	3	7	15	35
Giant White Stuttgart, grows to an enormous size, white, juicy, large as a turnip	3	7	15	40
Beckert's Chartier, almost transparent, large, extra fine quality, best radish grown	3	8	18	40
Rosy Gem, a beautiful turnip-shaped sort, crisp, tender,	3	8	18	40
White Box, white, turnip-shaped, early, solid and crisp, best for forcing,	3	8	18	40
White Strasburg, firm, brittle and tender, best long white for market	3	8	16	40
French Breakfast, mild, quick grower, oblong, popular	3	7	15	38

BECKERT'S CHARTIER.

	Pkt.	Oz.	¼lb.	lb.
White Turnip, similar to Scarlet Turnip except color	8¢	8¢	16	$ 38
Brll's Improved Long Scarlet, extra fine strain of the long scarlet	3	9	20	50
Early Round Dark Red, fine, for forcing, small tops, early, round, very dark red	3	8	16	40
White Lady Finger, rapid grower, crisp, brittle, tender, fine shape, desirable	4	9	20	45
Glass, the grand new forcing radish. Try it once for early	4	10	20	50

WINTER RADISHES.

Chinese Rose Winter, rose colored, best winter radish, large	3	7	15	45
California Mammoth Winter, long, white, large size	3	7	15	45
Black Spanish, the popular old variety	3	7	15	45

PARSNIPS.

Long Hollow Crown, best standard table and stock variety, long well-formed roots	3	7	14	35
Long Smooth White, roots long, smooth, white, sweet, tender, good keeper	3	7	14	35
Improved Guernsey, fine strain, heavy cropper, fine grained, excellent large variety	3	7	15	38

SQUASH.

Early Golden Summer Crookneck, best early standard summer variety	3	7	15	45
Giant Summer Crookneck, resembles the preceding but very large, fine quality	3	8	16	55
White Bush Scalloped, fine, early, good flavor, ships well	3	7	15	45
Red China, highly prized by many	3	8	18	45
Marblehead, dry, sweet and good keeper	3	7	15	45
Improved Hubbard, standard winter variety, best for general culture	3	7	15	45
Sibley, next to Hubbard as a winter variety, fine grained	3	7	15	45
Essex Hybrid, matures early for a winter variety, solid and large	3	7	15	45
Bay State, solid, heavy weight, firm, dry, sweet	3	7	15	45
Mammoth Chili, immense size, average 150 pounds each	3	8	20	60

THE FAXON SQUASH

Fordhook, earliest winter sort, keeps long, handsome in appearance, fine flavor, dry and sweet	4	10	25	75
Chicago Warty Hubbard, extra fine strain of Hubbard	5	12	30	90
Faxon, flesh deep orange, enormously productive, early, best quality, keeps long	4	10	25	75

SPINACH.

Round or Summer, standard early spring variety	3	6	10	20
Long Standing Thick Leaved, popular, slow to run to seed	3	6	10	20
Bloomsdale Savoy Leaved, popular where known	3	6	10	20
Prickly, or Fall, for fall sowing	3	7	12	30

TOMATOES.

	Pkt.	Oz.	¼lb.	lb.
Fordhook First, extra early, comes into market as soon as the extra early small rough tomatoes which possess no merit except earliness. Fordhook First is large, smooth, uniform in size and sells well (one-fifth ounce, 8¢)	5	30	90	2 15
Early Ruby, extra early, ripens in July, open growing plant, prolific	4	20	60	2 00
Golden Queen, popular with many golden yellow	3	15	50	1 65
Ponderosa, mammoth size, strong grower and productive	4	35	1 00	3 50
Mansfield's Tree, large size, good, can be trained up 10 or 12 feet	3	30	90	3 00
Atlantic Prize, extra early, good size productive	3	20	90	2 50
Perfection, good, solid, productive	3	15	50	1 75
Favorite, red, smooth, large, solid	3	15	50	1 75
Stone, extra heavy, solid, few seeds best late red for general crop	4	30	80	2 90
Dwarf Champion, compact tree-like growth, early, productive, red	3	18	55	1 85
Livingston's Beauty, enormous yielder, good shipper, popular	3	15	50	1 75
Acme, old standard, reddish purple color, good bearer	3	15	50	1 75
Trophy, late, well-known popular variety	3	15	50	1 75
Mayflower, one of the earliest of the large, glossy red tomatoes	3	15	50	1 75
Strawberry, or Winter Cherry, grows in small husks, productive, fine for preserves	4	25	85	3 00
Matchless, beautiful symetrical form, vigorous, rich red, solid, large	4	25	80	2 25
Mikado, productive, very large and early for size	3	20	60	1 75

TURNIPS, Flat or Field Varieties.

Name	Pkt.	Oz.	¼lb.	lb.
White Egg, desirable sort, white flesh, excellent table	3	7	15	35
Early White Flat Dutch, early, flat, quick grower	3	7	15	35
Large White Norfolk, large globe-shaped, later than most varieties, good keeper	3	7	15	35
Amber Globe, large, productive, yellow, globe-shaped	3	7	15	35
Improved Golden Ball, quick grower, very popular	3	7	15	35
Early Purple Top Munich, very early and good quality	3	7	15	35
Strap Leaf Purple Top, standard and most popular sort	3	7	15	35
White Globe, large, white, globe-shaped	3	7	15	35
Breadstone, fine quality, extra large and solid, good	3	8	20	60

STRAP LEAF PURPLE TOP.

SWEDE OR RUTA-BAGA TURNIPS

Name	Pkt.	Oz.	¼lb.	lb.
Sweet German, very fine quality, sweet	3	8	15	45
White Russian, best standard white, fine quality	3	7	15	40
Carter's Imperial Purple Top, best yellow flesh, globe shaped, fine quality	3	7	15	40
Bell's World's Fair, called the best purple-topped yellow ever introduced, large and smooth	3	7	15	45

Do not forget to add 8 cents to every pound and 15 cents to every quart of seed if you wish them sent by mail. Do not order a single pound or two by express; it will cost you more than if you add the postage and order by mail.

BELL'S WORLD'S FAIR.

HERBS.

This list comprises the most desirable varieties for seasoning soups meats, etc., and for medicinal purposes. Cut when dry just before they blossom, dry in the shade and pack in a tight box.

Any variety 3 cts. a packet; six or more packets at 2½ cts each.

Name.	Use	Oz.	¼lb.	Name.	Use	Oz.	¼lb.
Anise,—	Garnishes and seasoning	5	20	Marjoram, Sweet—	Seasoning	15	35
Balm,—	Balm tea and wine	20	75	Nigella Sativa,—	(Allspice)	15	40
Basil, Sweet—	Seasoning soups	20	75	Rosemary,—	Aromatic, seasoning	50	1 75
Caraway,—	Confectionery	8	25	Rue,—	Croup in fowls, medicinal	20	70
Catnip,—	Medical	40	1 50	Saffron,—	Medicinal, etc	15	50
Coriander,—	Garnishes, etc.	8	20	Sage,—	Seasoning, dressing	10	30
Dill,—	Soups and pickles	9	30	Sweet Fennell,—	Aromatic, fish sauce	10	35
Hoarhound,—	Seasoning, cough medicine	24	90	Summer Savory,—	Flavoring	10	30
Hyssop,—	Hyssop tea	15	50	Thyme,—	Seasoning, headache	30	1 00
Lavender,—	Aromatic and medical	10	30	Wormwood,—	Medicinal, for poultry	30	1 00

POTATOES.

COLUMBIA BEAUTY.

By cutting out the eyes of potatoes and mailing with a fair piece of the potato, you can, at a very small price, try all varieties. Six eyes of any one variety, by mail, 10¢; 20 eyes, not over four varieties, 25¢; 50 eyes, assorted as desired, 50¢; 100 eyes. 75¢; 1 lb., 20¢; 2 lbs., 35¢; 7 lbs., $1.00 Any of above by mail at prices quoted. Pecks and bushels by express, charges paid by purchaser. Bag of 90 lbs., any variety, $2.00.

	Peck	Bush
Early Puritan, extra fine and early, productive, resembles Early Rose but lighter, cooks very mealy	60¢	$1 40
Minister, dry, mealy, not very smooth	60	1 50
Stray Beauty, one of the best extra early, nearly round, good yielder. Dakota Red, late red, stocky grower, productive, excellent	55	1 35
	60	1 50
Rural New Yorker, No. 2, handsome, smooth, white, excellent quality, vigorous and productive	60	1 50
Columbia Beatuy, white, good yielder, mealy and dry, extra early and keeps well	70	1 75
Thorburns, very early and productive, excellent quality, desirable for market	60	1 75
Crown Jewell, thought to be unexcelled by many, good yielder	60	1 75
White Star, white, great yielder, unexcelled in many parts for main crop	60	1 40
Prolific Hug-Proof, the great productive late potato, vigorous grower, bugs seldom trouble vines extremely hardy, produces more potatoes to the acre than almost any other sort, good keeper	60	1 50
Rose of Erwin, this comparitively new potato has given the greatest satisfaction; It is a great yielder, fine quality, rather late, and just the potato for general market	75	1 75

SELECTED ✦ *FLOWER* ✦ SEEDS.

Our Flower Seeds comprise everything which is really worthy of general cultivation. In quality they are unsurpassed. The mixtures are made up of rare new varieties, and are much superior to the mixtures usually sold. Notice the low price at which we offer a package of seeds. Our packages contain as many seeds as those of other firms, and in many cases more.

☞ The number before each name is the catalogue number, and we can fill your order just as well if you simply write the number as we could were you to write out the name of the variety you want. The figures at the right are the prices in cents for a package of seeds.

Catalogue No.		Price per Package
1	**Abronia, Mixed.** Trailing, verbena-like plants, lilac and yellow flowers	3
3	**Abutilon, Fancy Mixed.** "Flowering Maple," beautiful house shrub; rare varieties only	8
4	" **Fireball.** Bushy, compact grower; deep crimson color .... (10 seeds)	10
6	" **Bell's Royal Chameleon.** golden variegated leaves; flowers intense scarlet. .(15 seeds)	20
7	**Acacia, Mixed.** Greenhouse shrub; graceful, foliage showy	8
8	**Achillea, Double White.** Profuse bloomer, hardy, fine for cemetery or cut flowers	8
12	**Acroclinum, Show Mixed.** Beautiful everlasting for winter bouquets; double and single	3
13	**Adlumia,** called Wood Fringe and Allegany Vine; very graceful climber with pinnate leaves	5
14	**Adonis, Mixed.** Red and scarlet, showy for borders, annuals	2
15	" **Vernalis.** Large showy yellow flowers, perennials	2
17	**Agapanthus, Umbellatus.** Handsome, 3 to 4 feet high, called African Lily	5
18	**Agave, Mixed.** highly interesting large succulent plants	5
19	**Ageratum, Lasseauxi.** Compact plant; blossoms pretty rose	4
19	" **Little Gem.** Compact; color most delicate blue	8
20	" **Little Dorrit.** Fine beautiful white	3
22	" **Swanley Blue.** Good bedder or house bloomer blue	3
26	" **Canary Yellow.** Compact; beautiful canary yel'w	3
21	" **Finest Mixed.** All choice varieties and colors	3
23	**Agrostemma, Fine Mixed.** Known as Rose of Heaven, ann'l	2
24	**Alonsoa, Mixed.** Shrub-like; will bloom in winter	2
25	**Allium, Mixed.** Lovely spring bloomer	4

AGERATUM, SWANLEY BLUE.

27	**Alyssum, Sweet.** Beautiful, white, fragrant flowers, will bloom in the house in winter	3
28	" **Little Gem.** Dwarf and spreading; covered with a mass of white flowers; a single plant has had 400 spikes of blossoms at a time	5
29	" **Floral Spray.** Resembles a mound of snow, profuse bloomer	4
30	" **Saxatile.** Hardy perennial; yellow flowers, called "Gold Dust"	3
31	**Amaranthus, Henderi.** Beautiful drooping foliage; crimson, orange, buff, etc.	4
32	" **Salicifolius.** "Fountain Plant;" magnificent plumes 3 to 4 ft. high	3
33	" **Bicolor.** Foliage changeable late in season	3
35	" **Nobilis Pyramidalis.** Grand, stately tropical plants, tapers to point	3
36	" **Tricolor,** "Joseph's Coat;" leaves red, yellow and green	2
37	" **Gibbosus.** Showy, long chains of dark bloom	3
38	" **Atropurpureus.** Blood red foliage, drooping flowers	3
39	" **Mixed.** Above and other choice varieties	2
40	**Ambrosia.** Long stems of fragrant, spray-like foliage	3
41	**Ammobium, Alatum Grandiflora.** Free flowering white annual, everlasting, very beautiful for winter bouquets	3
42	**Ampelopsis, Quinquefolia.** American Ivy, or Woodbine; rapid hardy climber	4
43	" **Veitchi.** Will cling to smooth wall; changes color in autumn	5
45	**Anchusa.** Resembles Forget-me-not; profuse bloomer	3
46	**Anemone.** Brilliant, hardy, spring-flowering plant; seeds sown in the spring will bloom in the house the following winter	3
48	**Antigonon.** Mexican Mountain Rose. Half hardy climber	4

Amaranthus Henderi.

49	**Antirrhinum or Snapdragon, Brilliant Mixed.** Beautiful hardy plant, blooming first season from seeds	3
51	**Arabis, Alpina.** Early and pretty spring flowers, pure white	3
52	**Aristolochia, Sipho.** Beautiful climber called Dutchman's Pipe Vine	10
55	**Aster, Harlequin.** Oddly and beautifully striped; blossoms very double	7
56	" **Peachblossom.** Large double flowers; lovely delicate tint, very desirable	8
57	" **Cocardean or Crown.** Showy, large double blossoms, center one color surrounding another	7
58	" **Fire Demon.** Beautiful pompone-flowered, blossoms of a fiery scarlet	7
59	" **Goliath.** Mammoth beautiful blossoms, of mixed colors	6
60	" **Hedge Hog or Needle.** Blossoms composed of long, needle-like petals of mixed colors	6
61	" **Mount Blanc.** Large, full white blossoms, very desirable for a white variety	6
62	" **Pæony Flowered.** Large and perfect form, pæony-shaped, great variety of colors	5
64	" **Rosa Flowered.** Large and double flowers resembling a rose, mixed colors	5
66	" **Washington.** One of the largest; flowers 4 to 5 inches in diameter, full and perfect	8
67	" **Pearl.** Dwarf globe-flowered, mixed colors	6
68	" **Comet.** Very novel, resembling a Japanese Chrysanthemum, large handsome flowers	10

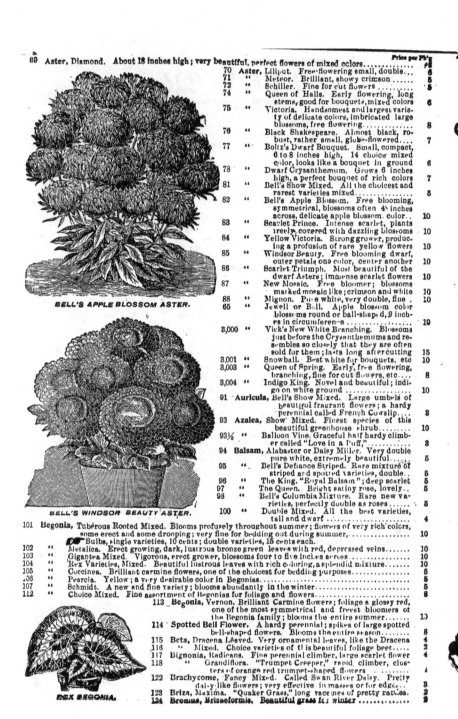

69 Aster, Diamond. About 18 inches high; very beautiful, perfect flowers of mixed colors............

Price per Pk'g

70 Aster, Liliput. Free-flowering small, double... 6
71 " Meteor. Brilliant, showy crimson...... 6
72 " Schiller. Fine for cut flowers......... 5
74 " Queen of Halls. Early flowering, long stems, good for bouquets, mixed colors 6
75 " Victoria. Handsomest and largest variety of delicate colors, imbricated large blossoms, free flowering............ 8
76 " Black Shakespeare. Almost black, robust, rather small, globe-flowered.... 7
77 " Boltz's Dwarf Bouquet. Small, compact, 6 to 8 inches high, 14 choice mixed color, looks like a bouquet in ground 6
78 " Dwarf Crysanthemum. Grows 6 inches high, a perfect bouquet of rich colors 7
81 " Bell's Show Mixed. All the choicest and rarest varieties mixed............ 5
82 " Bell's Apple Blossom. Free blooming, symmetrical, blossoms often 4 inches across, delicate apple blossom color.. 10
83 " Scarlet Prince. Intense scarlet, plants freely, covered with dazzling blossoms 10
84 " Yellow Victoria. Strong grower, producing a profusion of rare yellow flowers 10
85 " Windsor Beauty. Free blooming dwarf, outer petals one color, center another 10
86 " Scarlet Triumph. Most beautiful of the dwarf Asters; immense scarlet flowers 10
87 " New Mosaic. Free bloomer; blossoms marked mosaic like; crimson and white 10
88 " Mignon. Pure white, very double, fine . 10
65 " Jewell or Ball. Apple blossom color blossoms round or ball-shaped, 9 inches in circumference............ 10
3,000 " Vick's New White Branching. Blossoms just before the Crysanthemums and resembles so closely that they are often sold for them; lasts long after cutting 15
3,001 " Snowball. Best white for bouquets, etc 10
3,003 " Queen of Spring. Early, free flowering, branching, fine for cut flowers, etc. 8
3,004 " Indigo King. Novel and beautiful; indigo on white ground............ 10
91 Auricula, Bell's Show Mixed. Large umbels of beautiful fragrant flowers; a hardy perennial called French Cowslip.... 8
93 Azalea, Show Mixed. Finest species of this beautiful greenhouse shrub......... 10
93½ " Balloon Vine. Graceful half hardy climber called "Love in a Puff," 8
94 Balsam, Alabaster or Daisy Miller. Very double pure white, extremely beautiful..... 5
95 " Bell's Defiance Striped. Rare mixture of striped and spotted varieties, double.. 5
96 " The King. "Royal Balsam"; deep scarlet 5
97 " The Queen. Bright satiny rose, lovely.. 5
98 " Bell's Columbia Mixture. Rare new varieties, perfectly double as roses 5
100 " Double Mixed. All the best varieties, tall and dwarf............ 4
101 Begonia, Tuberous Rooted Mixed. Blooms profusely throughout summer; flowers of very rich colors, some erect and some drooping; very fine for bedding out during summer,............... 10
☞ Bulbs, single varieties, 10 cents; double varieties, 15 cents each.
102 " Metalica. Erect growing, dark, lustrous bronze green leaves with red, depressed veins....... 10
103 " Gigantea Mixed. Vigorous, erect grower, blossoms four to five inches across............ 10
104 " Rex Varieties, Mixed. Beautiful lustrous leaves with rich coloring, a splendid mixture....... 10
105 " Coccinea. Brilliant carmine flowers, one of the choicest for bedding purposes....... 5
106 " Pearcia. Yellow; a very desirable color in Begonias............ 5
107 " Schmidt. A new and fine variety; blooms abundantly in the winter............ 5
112 " Choice Mixed. Fine assortment of Begonias for foliage and flowers............ 8
113 Begonia, Vernon. Brilliant Carmine flowers; foliage a glossy red, one of the most symmetrical and freest bloomers of the Begonia family; blooms the entire summer....... 10
114 Spotted Bell Flower. A hardy perennial; spikes of large spotted bell-shaped flowers. Blooms the entire season............ 8
115 Beta, Dracena Leaved. Very ornamental leaves, like the Dracena 4
116 " Mixed. Choice varieties of this beautiful foliage beet..... 2
117 Bignonia, Radicans. Fine perennial climber, large scarlet flower 4
118 " Grandiflora. "Trumpet Creeper," rapid, climber, clusters of orange red trumpet-shaped flowers . 4
122 Brachycome, Fancy Mixed. Called Swan River Daisy. Pretty daisy-like flowers; very effective in masses or for edges... 5
123 Briza, Maxima. "Quaker Grass," long race mes of pretty rattles. 3
124 Bromus, Brizaeformis. Beautiful grass for winter............ 3

BELL'S APPLE BLOSSOM ASTER.

BELL'S WINDSOR BEAUTY ASTER.

REX BEGONIA.

SNOW QUEEN CANDYTUFT.

CALCEOLARIA.

MARGARITAE CARNATION.

CANTERBURY BELL

125 **Browallia, Mixed. Tender** plants, rich, winged blossoms, freely produced... 3
127 **Cactus,** Cereus Mixed. Choice varieties such as Night-blooming Cereus................. 15
128 " Choice Mixed. Rare mixture of 150 choice varieties.......... 15
129 **Caladium,** New Sorts Mixed. Gorgeously colored ornamental leaves, 10 seed 10
133 **Calceolaria,** Painted Margin. Beautiful margined varieties of these rare pocket-shaped flowers.. 10
134 " Fancy Mixed. Great assortment of these beautiful flowers... 10
135 " Shrubby Dwarf. Pretty, shrublike plants for greenhouses 10
136 **Calendula,** Meteor. Large beautifully imbricated double flowers 3
137 " Prince of Orange. Florets striped more intense than Meteor, profuse bloomer.. 4
138 **Calendula,** Double White. Large, choice and distinct white variety 4
139 " Choice Mixed. All the best varieties 3
140 **Calla,** Aethiopica. Seeds will produce small Calla bulbs by fall..... 10
141 **Calliopsis,** Golden Wave. The best yellow flower grown for cut flowers or masses; covered with hundreds of brilliant and effective blossoms 2 inches across, from July to October 3
142 " Golden King. Dwarf, abundant bloomer, yellow margin with maroon center............................. 3
143 " New Double. Choice double varieties in mixture, showy 4
144 " Finest Mixed. Our mixture includes all showy varieties 3
146 **Cherianthus,** Fairy Queen. Bright maltese cross blossoms borne in profusion on spikes, blossoms in a month after sowing 3
147 **Camellia,** Japonica, Double Mixed. These beautiful shrubs are admired for their brilliant flowers and glossy green leaves, growing from seed is the only way to get new varieties .. 10
148 **Campanula,** Fine Mixed. A rare assortment of these beautiful bell-shaped flowers, all colors.......................... 3
150 " Pyramidalis. Grand plant called Pyramidal Bell Flower 4
151 " Cup and Saucer. Hardy biennial, beautiful colored blossoms resembling cup and saucer.................... 4
152 **Canary Bird Flower.** One of the most beautiful and rapid of the annual climbers; covered with a profusion of canary-colored blossoms resembling the bird's expanded wings 4
153 **Candytuft,** New Empress. Giant form of the Rocket Candytuft; produces trusses of flowers 4 to 8 inches long which almost resemble hyacinths................ 5
154 " Snow Queen. Distinct species, very beautiful, bloom almost the entire season, completely covering the the ground with its tufts of white blossoms 4
156 " Rocket. Pure white blossoms in long spikes (oz. 20¢) 3
157 " Carmine. Very choice and showy 3
158 " Dark Crimson. Makes a good show.............. 3
160 " Mixed. All choice; good for bouquets and cut oz. 20¢ 2
161 " Sempervirens. "Evergreen White Candytuft,"...... 3
163 **Canna,** Mixed. Large stately plants, 4 to 6 ft. high........... 3
164 " Warszewiczii. Lovely bright red flowers, striped foliage 4
167 " Dark and Red Leaved Sorts. Fine mixture best dark 4
169 " Crozy's or Gladiolus. Magnificent large flowering strain, blossoms large as gladiolus, more brilliant, colors run through all desirable shades, start seed in house and they will bloom in July or August.. 10
170 **Canterbury Bell,** Double Mixed. One of the most beautiful and popular biennial plants; flowers richly colored 3
171 " Single Mixed. Very showy and beautiful......... 3
172 " New Striped. Beautiful striped double variety.... 4
173 **Carnation.** Double Mixed. Deliciously fragrant rare and beautiful colors, for the house or open ground............ 5
174 " Grenadin. Dark varieties, mixed.. 10
175 " Remontant or Tree. Winter flowers 10
178 " Margaritae. Beautiful class of perpetual blooming Carnations, will bloom in 3 to 4 months from sowing, beautiful colors............. 10
181 **Celastrus.** Scandens. Hardy climber, grows 20 feet high, blossoms early, scarlet berries on vine all winter; called "Bitter Sweet."..... 4
183 **Celosia.** Mixed Curious ornamental heads of blossoms called Cockscomb......... 3

GLASGOW PRIZE CELOSIA.

184 **Celosia.** Glasgow Prize. Very fine pot plant; dwarf and showy 4
186 **Centurea,** Victoria One of the most showy novelties ever introduced for a garden or pot plant. Blooms in 80 days from sowing seed 5

CINERARIA.

☞ The above varieties are the winter blooming Chrysanthemums.

☞ The following Chrysanthemums are annuals and suitable for summer flowering in open ground.

CLARK's 4.

☞ All varieties of Clematis are rapid, hardy climbers.

CLEMATIS CRIPSA.

DAHLIA.

227
228

CUPHEA.

CYCLAMEN.

250 **Cuphea,** Miniata. Rich vermilion and violet 5
251 " Mixed. Fiery red and crimson, brown 5
252 " Bell's Show Mixed. Choice strains of these beautiful house plants...................... 10
253 **Cyclamen,** Giant Mixed. Mixture of the extra choice varieties of this grand greenhouse plant. Plants bloom from fall to spring; blossoms delicate and beautiful colors, will bloom by winter from seed sown in spring 10
254 **Cyclanthera,** Explodens. Pretty vine; fruit explodes with a loud noise........................ 3
256 **Cyperus,** Alternifolius. Umbrella Plant. Pretty foliage...... 3
257 **Cypress Vine,** Mixed. Beautiful, delicate annual climber, grows 15 ft. high and blooms profusely 3
258 **DAHLIAS,** Rosalind Mixture. Seeds saved only from rare new double Dahlias 15
259 " New Single Mixed. Choice single varieties 5
260 " Gracilis. Choice striped variety................. 5
261 " Liliputian. Beautiful dwarf double............. 10
262 " Double Selected Mixed. All choice double varieties 10
263 " Zimpani. Dwarf black 5
264 " Cactus. The finest possible sorts of double, new.. 15
265 **DAISY,** Double Mixed. (Bellis Perennis.) As desirable for borders, etc., as pansies; fine for small bouquets; blooms from early spring until frost............. 5
266 " Constant, or Ball of Snow. Double pure white...... 8
267 " Longfellow. Blossoms on long stems, best for bouquets double dark rose 10
268 **Datura,** Wrightii. (Angel's Trumpet.) Trumpet-shaped flowers, white, passing into lilac.................. 3
269 " Double Mixed. Magnificent, fragrant and stately... 4
271 **Delphinum,** Chinese Mixed. (Hardy Larkspur.) Handsome long spikes of beautiful bloom............... 3
272 " New Hybrids Mixed. All rare new varieties...... 4
273 " Formosium. Rich blue, grows 2 feet high......... 3
274 " Sulphureum (New Yellow Orchid Lark-pur.) Extremely rare, new, resembles yellow Orchids.... 10
275 **Delphinum,** Pillar of Beauty. Delicate azure blue, spikes 2 ft. long, fine.... 5

See our grand Dianthus Pinks on colored page.

296 **Dictamnus** Praxinella. (Burning Bush or Gas Plant.) Hardy bushy plant; fragrant flowers, gives off a flashy vapor on warm evenings.......... 5
297 **Digitalis,** Show Mixed. (Fox Glove.) Thimble-shaped blossoms in spikes.. 3
298 **Dodecatheon,** Clevelandi. (Giant American Cowslip.) Hardy, flowers Cyclamen like in bunches, very handsome 8
299 **Dolichos,** Lablab. The ornamental climber, Hyacinth Bean 2
300 " Atrosanguineus. (Blood-Red Egyptian Bean.) Fine annual climbing vine; vine red, blossoms rose, seed-pods blood-red 4
302 **Escheveria,** Fancy Mixed. Pretty for house or rockeries 10
304 **Eragrostis,** Elegans. (Love Grass.) Beautiful dancing spikelets, handsome 3
305 **Erianthus,** Ravennae. Ornamental grass 9 to 11 ft. high, resembles Pampas grass and plumes but is much larger..................... 4
306 **Erica.** (Cape Heath.) Pretty house shrub..................... 4
307 **Eritrichium,** Barbigerum. Free flowering white 3
300 **Erythrina,** Crista-Galli. (Brazilian Coral Plant.)................ 5
310 **Eschscholtzia,** Finest Mixed. (California Poppy.) Brilliant and fine........ 3
311 **Eulalia,** Japonica Zebrina. Handsome striped grass, 5 to 6 feet high, spikes resemble ostrich plumes 5
312 **Four-o'clock,** or Marvel of Peru, Finest Mixed. Old annual, beautiful, loaded with blossoms after 4 p.m 2
313 **Euphorbia,** Variegata. Pretty "Snow on the Mountain 3
314 **Freesia,** Fancy Mixed. Pretty winter bloomer...... 5
316 **Fuchsia,** Finest Mixed. Choice, well known plants.. 10
317 " Double Mixed. Rare double sorts [15 seeds]. 10
318 " Procumbens. (Trailing Fuchsia.) Pretty hanging basket plant; blossoms profusely and trails over edge of pot; bright red berries fills the plant after blossoms have faded. [12 seeds] 10
321 **Gallardia,** Show Mixed. Showy annual, blooms early from seed sown in spring, and lavishes its gay flowers until the frosts 3
322 **Geranium,** Apple-Scented. Pretty, fragrant, 12 seeds 10
323 " Rose Scented. Choice......[15 seeds].... 10
324 " Fancy-Leaved Sorts, Mixed. Only the rarest sorts of gold, white, bronze and variegated leaves....[12 seeds]......... 15
325 " Large Flowering, Mixed. Seeds only from large flowering or grandiflora sorts, very choice...................[12 seeds]. 15
326 " Ivy-Leaved, Double and single, [12 seeds].... 15
327 **Geranium,** French Blotched or Odier. Large flowering with blotched petals........... [12 seeds].... 15
328 " Fancy Mixed. All sorts in mixture 10
329 **Gesneria,** Fancy Mixed. Lovely house flower, resembles Gloxinias..................... 10
331 **Gladiolus,** Fancy Mixed. All choice varieties............................. 3

DAHLIA. Rosalind Mixture.

BALL-OF-SNOW DAISY.

GLOXINIA.

GODETIA.

HOLLYHOCKS.

LANTANA.

| 421 | Mimulus, | Queen's Prize. Grand flowering pot plant............................ | 8 |

421 **Mimulus,** Queen's Prize. Grand flowering pot plant.. 8
422   "   Hose in Hose. Two beautifully spotted trumpets inserted one within the other, grand.·· 10
423   "   Bell's Show Mixed. All the grand varieties................................ 8
424   "   Mixed. All varieties.. 5
425 **Mirabilis,** Multiflora. Triangular and somber foliage; a pretty, circular bush producing its bouquets
     of grand violet blossoms from June until the frosts come................................. 10
426   "   Tom Thumb. Best dwarf varieties mixed..................................... 2
427 **Molucca Balm, or Shell Flower.** Curious, pretty and interesting........ 5
428 **Momordica.** A rapid climber, with yellow, transparent fruit............. 4
429 **Moon Flower.** A popular, rapid climber; blossoms 3 to 6 inches in diam-
     eter; grows 25 to 40 feet in a season................................. 8
431 **Musa Ensete.** The beautiful, rapid-growing "Abyssinian Banana Tree".. 10
433 **Myostis or Forget-me-not.** Sweet little plant; blooms early in spring.. 5
435   "   "   "   Victoria. Best for edges; azure blue, round,
     7 inches high................................. 8
436 **Narcissus.** Pretty old spring flowers................................ 5
437 **Dwarf Nasturtium,** Empress of India. Dark leaves and crimson flowers 4
438   "   "   Crimson.. 3
439   "   "   Rose. Soft rose... 3
440   "   "   Yellow.. 3
441   "   "   Spotted. Beautiful.. 3
442   "   "   Beauty. Canary and scarlet............................. 3
443   "   "   Scarlet. Flashing scarlet.................................. 3
444   "   "   Crystal Palace Gem. Sulphur and maroon.............. 3
445   "   "   King of Tom Thumbs. One of the finest crimson sorts... 4
446   "   "   King Theodore. Dark maroon............................ 4

MACHET MIGNONETTE

447 **Dwarf Nasturtium,** Golden King. Exquisite yellow .. 8
448   "   "   Coerlueo Roseum. Beautiful peach color 8
449   "   "   Bronze King. Changeable crimson bronze 4
450   "   "   Aurora. Chrome-yellow ground, upper
     petals lighter, two lower spotted, veined 8
451   "   "   Gold-Leaved. Foliage bright yellow, and
     scarlet flowers; handsome and compact 8
452   "   "   White Pearl. Very fine white........... 8
453   "   "   Tom Thumb Lady Bird. Orange, and red 8
3018   "   "   Ruby King. New, ruby red, large, fine.. 5
3019   "   "   Minus. Half the size of ordinary Nastur-
     tium; dainty and fine for edgings, etc.. 5
454   "   "   Tom Thumb, Dwarf Mixed. All above.. 8
     [oz. 20¢ ; ⅓oz. 10¢ ; ¼ lb. 50¢]
One packet each above varieties dwarf Nasturtiums, 60c.

55 **Climbing Nasturtiums,** Purple and Gold. Golden
     yellow foliage, rich purple flowers 4
456   "   "   Dunnet's Orange. Dark orange..... 2
457   "   "   Edward Otto. Silky bronze......... 2
458   "   "   Pearl. Very delicate................ 4
459   "   "   Coccineum. Scarlet 2
460   "   "   Striped Varieties. Assorted. 3
461   "   "   Regelianum. Violet crimson......... 2
462   "   "   Schillingi. Bright yellow.......... 2
701   "   "   Von Moltke. Beautiful rose 3
723   "   "   Brown King. Showy brown......... 3
463   "   "   Mixed. All colors [oz. 15c. ¼ lb. 40c.] 2
One packet each above varieties Climbing Nasturtiums 25c.

LADY BIRD NASTURTIUM.

464 **Tropæolum Lobbianum,** Mixed. Quick growing and
     profuse bloomer, brilliant, rich, blooms winter 4
465 **Primrose Nasturtium,** Asa Gray. Beautiful summer
     flowering, delicate primrose blossoms produc-
     ed in great profusion.... 5
466 **Nemophila,** Fine Mixed. Delicate and pretty plants,
     blotched and spotted annuals................ 5
467 **Nerium or Oleander,** Mixed. Showy plant, fine flowers 5
468 **Nicotiana,** Affinis. Handsome, tube shaped, white
     flowers, blooms in 3 months from sowing 4
469   "   Macrophylla. Stately, large, red flowers 4
470 Nicotiana, Decurrens. Dwarf, branching, large white fragrant flowers..... 4
471 Nigella, Damascena. Known as "Love in a Mist," "Lady in Green," etc..... 2
472 Nolana, Mixed. Pretty annual trailer for hanging baskets or out doors... 2
473 Nymphæa, Double White Water Lily. Grows readily from seed sown in
     pots covered with water................................ 5
474   "   Zanzibariensis The "Royal Purple Water Lily." Very fragrant 15
475   "   Red. Large and fine................................ 15
476   "   Lotus. Magnificent; white suffused with red................. 15
One packet of each of the above four Water Lillies, 40 cts,

477 **Œnothera,** Mixed. The showy "Evening Primrose,"........................ 3
478   "   Mexicana. The "Mexican Primrose,".............................. 5
479   "   Chilian Primrose. Prostrate growing, saucer-shaped, satiny white 5
480 Oxalis, Mixed. Pretty trailing plants for hanging baskets.................. 10
532 Passiflora, Coerulea. The best hardy Passion Flower; handsome climber... 5
535   "   Mammoth. Handsome large flowering.................... 10
536 Pentstemone, Mixed Varieties. Beautiful spikes of rich bloom, hardy plant 4
538 Perilla. Handsome plant for foliage, near y equals Coleus................ 3
539 Phacelia, Mixed. Good in bouquets, fine for bees...................... 3
540 **Phlox, Hardy,** Bell's Show Mixed. Best hardy border plant; magnificent varieties 5

MYOSTIS.   **EMPRESS OF INDIA.**

NICOTIANA AFFINIS.

GAY DIANTHUS PINKS.

Price par Pk'g

276	**Mourning Cloak.** Dark purple, nearly black; tips of petals pure white, very double, exceedingly fine	5
277	**Diadematus Pienissimus.** Very double, pink center, covered with Chinese-like hieroglyphics	4
278	**Heddewigii fl. pl.** (*Heddewig's Pink.*) Large and double half-hardy biennial; varied brilliant colors	5
279	**Japanese Pink.** Striped and fringed	5
280	**The Bride, or Little Gem.** Very dwarf, compact, bushy; large flowers of magnificent brilliant colors	5
281	**Laciniatus fl. pl.** (*Double Japan.*) Half-hardy biennial; rich in hue, very double; indiscribable beauty	6
282	**Diadematus,** (*Double Diadem.*) Dwarfish; very regular, densely double, and of all rich tints	4
283	**Eastern Queen.** Magnificent single flowers, 2 to 4 inches across, beautifully striped and stained	4
284	**Double Yellow.** A choice novel color	4
285	**Snowflake.** Extra large white flowers, beautifully fringed, single	4
286	**Imperiallis fl. pl.** (*Double Imperial.*) A superb double variety [oz. 45¢]	4
287	**Laciniatus.** Beautiful, large, single flowers, handsomely fringed	3
288	**Plumarius.** "Feathered Garden or Pleasant Eyed Pink;" large, fragrant, single flowers	3
289	**New "Cyclops."** New and very novel, clove-like fragrance, robust, free-blooming, blooms 1st season	10
290	**Deltoides.** The beautiful perennial "Maiden Pink," blossoms rose-colored with dark circle	3
291	**Double White.** Flowers large, pure white and very double	3
292	**Dwarf Double.** Very fine; mixture of double dwarf varieties [oz. 50¢]	3
293	**Striatus.** Beautiful double, large, full and exquisitely striped, one of the most showy	4
294	**Bell's Show Mixture.** Our selection of the finest strains, selected and put up by us	4
295	**Fine Mixed.** All choice varieties [oz. 40¢, ¼ oz. 10¢]	4
739	**Crimson Belle.** Very showy; a nearly new variety	3
3036	**Henderson's "Crown of Perfection."** Very large and densely double, blooms freely, wonderful diversity of rich colors, easily grown, seeds sown in the open ground in spring will bloom in summer	10

BEAUTIFUL VERBENAS.

663	**Lemon Verbena.** The delightful fragrance of its leaves makes this variety indispensible for bouquets			6
664	**New Golden-Leaved.** Intense blossoms contrasting finely with the golden yellow foliage, effective			15
665	**Dwarf Hybrids.** Dwarf and compact; flowers large and well matched, four choice colors mixed			15
666	**Large Flowering Verbena.** Known as "Mammoth Verbena." Vigorous grower, large flower trusses			8
667	**Odorata, or Sweet Scented.** Pinkish white flowers in spikes; very sweet scented and free bloomer			6
668	**Oculata.** Large, well-defined eyes of harmonious blended shades; strong and free bloomers			8
669	**Bell's Show Mixed.** Seeds saved only from choice specimens; of rich color and good form and size			8
670	**Finest Scarlet.** Blossoms intense scarlet	8	689	**Montana.** Hardy old variety	5
671	**Italian Striped.** Carnation-like stripes	8	673	**Finest Mixed.** All choice varieties	5
672	**White.** Pure white, true in color	8			

GRAND AND GORGEOUS PETUNIAS.

780	**Inimitable.** Compact, dwarf growing; well adapted to massing, etc	4
781	**Finest Striped and Blotched.** Beautifully veined and blotched, very showy	4
782	**Bell's Show Mixture.** Includes all the choicest single varieties	4
783	**Fine Mixed.** Best varieties for summer flowering in the open ground	3

LARGE FLOWERING PETUNIAS.

784	**Grandiflora Mixed.** Choicest large varieties	10	787	**Lady of the Lake,** Double; white corollas	15
785	**Grandiflora Quadricolor.** Large; splendid	10	788	**Double Fringed.** Full and finely fringed	15
880	**Bell's Inimitable:** Blossoms large and distinct; edges finely toothed, cut or plain		778	**Double Mixed:** Choice and selected double	10
			779	**Bell's Inimitable Double.** Rarest varieties	15
	Finest mixture of large single grandiflora	10	776	**California Giant:** Mammoth size, single mix'd	15

DOUBLE FLOWERING PETUNIAS.

STOCK,—GILLY FLOWER.

640	**Ten Weeks Stock,** Mixed Colors. Very choice selection	8
641	**Perpetual Flowering,** Extremely free-flowering; has fine habits	10
642	**Wall Flower Leaved,** Ten choice colors mixed	10
643	**Bromton or Winter Stock,** Twelve choice colors mixed	10
644	**New Stock, White Perfection,** Branching; white flowers; very valuable	10
645	**Blood Red Bouquet,** Very choice; one of the sweetest bouquet-like plants	10
1344	**Rose Bouquet,** Companion of Blood Red Bouquet; both dwarf free bloomers	10
1345	**New Perpetual Flowering, Peach Blossom:** Unusually lovely and delicate	10

ZINNIAS.

794	**New Pompone,** Mixed Colors. Half ordinary size, most vivid colors, showy	5
793	**Selected Dwarf,** Extra fine strains of symmetrical, dwarf free-flowering	5
795	**Zebra,** Finely striped blossoms, many new colors; one of the most choice	5
796	**Mammoth,** Extra large, very double, assorted colors mixed	5
797	**Double Mixed,** All choice colors	3
1316	**New Zinnia, Curled and Crested:** A rare class; very double, and curled	8

SIX GRAND NOVELTIES FOR 50 cts.

TEN WEEKS STOCK

NEW DOUBLE MORNING GLORY. Grand climber; same as single except with lovely double blossoms. Per packet, 10 cts.

JAPANESE MORNING GLORY, Magnificent free-flowering climber; blossoms of mammoth size: strange gaudy colors. Per pk't 15c.

PETUNIA, GIANT OF CALIFORNIA. Magnificent blossoms 4 to 5 inches across. Grand, choice colors. Per packet, 15 cts.

NEW PERPETUAL CARNATION. (Grace Guilland.) Finest Carnation; abundant bloomer. Per packet, 15 cts.

DATURA, CORNUCOPIA. (Horn of Plenty.) Blossoms 8 in. long; grandest plant ever produced; delightfully fragrant; bears 200 to 300 blossoms in a season. Per packet, 15c.

NEW RICINUS. Zanzibariensis: Gigantic, and surpassing Palma Christa; fan leaves 2 ft. and over long and of gay colors; grows from seed in a few months. Per packet, 10 cts.

❋ FLORAL NOVELTIES. ❋

NEW DWARF GOLDEN YELLOW PEA.

AN exquisitely beautiful annual, with blossoms of a rich yellow color, The blossoms are as large as the new large flowering Sweet Peas, and resemble them in form. They are produced in racemes Fox Glove style, with thirty to fifty blossoms on a spike.

It blooms profusely throught the summer and until killed by frost.

The plant is low, and branching sends up numerous spikes. Its leaves are oval and a beautiful dark green.

Price per packet...................... 10¢

3 packets,........................... 25¢

NEW DWARF SWEET PEA,
"CUPID."

" CUPID " grows only about five inches high, with flowers as large as Emily Henderson and of a pure white.

❋⊕❋

A field of these Peas looks at first like a green mass of cypress, but it soon changes to a mass of white. It is equally as fragrant and as

beautiful as any sweet peas, and surpasses others in abuudance of bloom, ease of culture and the uses to which it may be put. The plant is upright and has no tendency to trail. Its height seldom exceeds six inches, and yet it always bears a thrifty, vigorous appearance. At first it pushes up a central stem and then side stems are pushed out, thus giving it a spreading, bushy look, making it unnecessary to plant seeds nearer than six inches apart. The plants are equally as hardy as the tall growing Sweet Peas, and from their method of growth must soon be acknowledged as far superior. It blooms from early in the season until cut down by frost. The blossoms are three on a stem, and all open at once. No one should miss trying this great novelty this season.

Price, by mail, post paid:—1 packet, 15¢ ; 2 packets, 25¢ ; 10 packets, $1.00.

One package of the BEAUTIFUL SWEET PEA SHRUB, so popular with many, price 10¢ a package, will be given free to anyone sending 25c. for 1 package of each of the above two grand novelties. This is a magnificent offer; do not miss it.

CATALOGUE of IMPROVED
SELECTED SEEDS.

J. J. BELL CO., BINGHAMTON, New York.

Growers, Importers and Dealers in
:——IMPROVED AND PERFECTED SEEDS.——:

The J. J. BELL CO. is a consolidation of several seed firms. the largest of which was the well-known Seed House of J. J. Bell. It was organized in Dec., 1896, with a capital stock of $140,000.00, for the purpose of handling new and improved strains of seeds suitable for all localities. A study has been made of all varieties and those best adapted to early, medium and late planting, selected with a view to offering in a simple practical manner a list which while complete, would not confuse the purchaser with a long useless lot of names, each called the best. It will be the aim of the proprietors to make the list as short as possible, and yet have the best. When dealing with us you can rely on one thing—that our Extra Early is the BEST EARLY our Medium the BEST MEDIUM; our Late the BEST LATE. We do not claim that our varieties are all new; for example, if we fail to find a better early Beet than Mitchell's Early Turnip, and we fail to improve that, we should use that for our Early Turnip Beet. Our seeds are the best improved strains of the best sorts now in cultivation, and we have tried to make the prices low enough to compete as far as possible with the Cheap John, trashy seeds offered by some firms, and thus induce you to deal with us.

All seeds mailed free at catalogue prices, except those marked by express. If you order by express deduct 4c. postage for half pints, 16c, for quarts, 2c. for quarter pounds and 8c. for pounds.
Price of all seeds where price is not given is 4c. a packet; 10 or more packets 3c. each

Asparagus—EARLY MAMMOTH, Large, uniform size, early; shoots one to two inches in diameter, rapid grower. ½oz. 8c, oz. 14c, ¼ lb. 45c, lb. $1.25.

Beans.
BUSH.

Packets of Beans 4c. each, and contain about two ounces of seed. An ordinary garden should have about half a pint.

Extra Early Golden Pod Wax or Butter—The best early sort for family or market, good yielder, stringless and fine quality; extra early and does not rust. ½ pt. 12c, qt. 38c.

Rust Proof Wax or Butter—Beans black, strong erect grower, productive, tender and excellent quality; early, vigorous, holds pods well off the ground, and is almost absolutely rust proof. ½ pint 14c, qt. 40c.

Medium Wax—Long yellow pods, handsome and immensely productive, wonderfully vigorous, pods unexcelled for size and for beautiful color, fine for string or early shelled bean. ½ pt. 14c, qt. 40c.

Early Green Pod—Very early, productive and a good string variety. ½ pint 10c, quart 35c.

EXTRA EARLY GREEN POD.

Lima Bush—Productive and earlier than the pole Limas; gives you a good supply of Lima beans without the trouble and expense of poles. ½ pt. 15c, qt. 45c.

White Marrowfat—Best late white shelled bean, good yielder for field crop. ½ pt. 10c, quart 30c.

Yosemite Mammoth Wax, The Yosemite Bean is of such gigantic growth that really a small quantity of seed will go farther than than an ordinary bush bean. This is the prototype of a new race of wax bush beans. The name was suggested for this splendid bean on account of its enormous size. The pods frequently attain a length of ten to fourteen inches and are nearly all solid pulp, the seeds being very small when the pods are fit for use. The pods are a rich golden color and absolutely stringless, cooking tender and delicious. This is the coming wax bean for family or market purposes. It is enormously productive, as many as fifty of its enormous pods having been counted on one bush. ½ pint 20c, qt. 75c.

EXTRA EARLY GOLDEN WAX.

☞ Remember at the prices given we send quarts, pounds and all smaller quantities by mail post paid. If your order is large you could have them sent by express or freight and pay the express or freight charges at you depot and thus save the postage which is 8 cents a pound and 16 cents a quart and at the same rate for smaller quantities. Deduct this amount paid for postage if you order by express or freight.

POLE BEANS.

Early Cluster Wax. Very early productive, grows in immense clusters, poles will be crowded with great clusters of beautiful yellow pods for 10 ft. ½ pint, 15c., quart 45c.

Prolific Green Pod. Very productive, fine quality, tender, stringless and melting, cooks well. ½ pt. 15c, quart, 45c.

Bell's Pole Lima. Large beans, vigorous, fine quality, great yielder, earlier than most Limas. ½pt, 15c, quart, 45c.

Andalusia Wax. The grandest and most wonderful pole bean ever offered. Often yields one half bushel of large, luscious, rich yellow pods at one picking Pods are broad, fleshy and entirely stringless, of unsurpassed flavor and commence to bear very young, producing its crop lavishly throughout the entire season. Packet, 6c, 2 pkts. 10c. ½ pt. 20c, quart, 50c. (See Cut)

NEW GOLDEN ANDALUSIA BEAN

Early Cluster Wax.

A SINGLE PICKING FROM ONE VINE

½ BUSHEL

BEET.

Extra Early Red Turnip. Very early, perfect form, deep dark red. fine grained, extra table qualities, has small top and will stand close planting. Does not get tough and woody. Oz. 9c., ¼ lb. 20c., lb. 65c.

Medium Blood Turnip. Good for general crop or for winter use; good size and keeps well, quality good, crisp and tender, best where a good winter sort is desired. Oz. 8c., ¾ lb. 16c., lb. 45c

Improved Sugar. Immense yielder, will produce about as much as the Mangle Wurtzel; very sweet and fine for stock feeding or sugar making; good for the table. Oz. 8c, ¼ lb. 15c., lb. 40c.

MANGLE WURTZEL BEET

Golden Tankard. Very nutritious and a great milk producer; yields as high as 75 tons per acre and is unexcelled for stock feeding, being nearly as fine quality as a table beet. Oz. 7c., ¼ lb. 15c., lb. 40c.

Prize Long Red. Mammoth size, the best red mangle wurtzel grown, produces an immense crop. Oz. 8c., ¼ lb. 15c lb. 40c.

Golden Tankard Mangel Wurtzel.

CABBAGE.

Our Cabbage is the finest strain American grown and can be relied upon as being the very best.

Early Winningstadt. Best early for garden or home use; surest header of all, very hard, heavy and solid, will weigh as much as a large flat cabbage and is equally as desirable to sow late for winter use; fine flavor. Oz. 12c., ¼ lb. 35c., lb. $1.25.

Early Jersey Wakefield. Selected strain of extra early improved size and compact sure heading quality. This is the most popular sort for early market growers. ½ oz. 8c., oz. 15c., ¼ lb. 50c., lb. $1.75.

Bell's Second Early. Good sized heads, flatish in form, market just behind the Wakefield and is unsurpassed as an early summer sort. ½ oz. 8c., oz. 15c., ¼ lb. 50c., lb. $2.00.

CABBAGE—continued.

Bell's Medium. Almost every plant makes a good saleable head of large size and a little rounder than the Flat Dutch. Fine quality and unsurpassed for a fall cabbage. Try this once and you will grow no other. ½ oz. 8c., oz. 15c., ¼ lb. 55c, lb. $2.00.

Premium Flat Dutch. Well-known, standard, late crop cabbage; heads large and flat, good shape for market and always sells well, keeps well Oz. 12c., ¼ lb. 45c., lb. $1.50.

Improved Winter Header. Very large heads, late, good quality, unequalled keeping qualities, dark green, can be planted closer than most large sorts as it has fewer outer leaves. ½ oz. 10c. oz. 18c., ¼ lb. 60c., lb. $2.25.

Bell's Surehead. Nearly every plant forms a large solid head of perfect form, making it a good shipper. It has few outer leaves and can be planted close. The quality is unsurpassed, and it is all around the best cabbage for late planting in private gardens. ½ oz. 10c., oz. 18c, ¼ lb. 60c., lb. $2.25.

EARLY WINNINGSTADT.

IMPROVED WINTER HEADER.

BELL'S SUREHEAD.

CARROTS.

Extra Early Forcing. Small but grows very quickly, so is desirable for an extra early sort. Oz. 8c, ¼ lb. 22c., lb. 75c.

Improved Oxheart. Also called Guerande—Best medium sized sort, excellent for table use and a sure cropper. Oz. 9c., ¼ lb. 24c., lb. 80c.

Improved Long Orange. Long, large roots of a uniform size and rich deep yellow color, growing one foot long and from two to three inches in diameter. Good keeper and fine for table use or stock feeding. Oz. 8c, ¼ lb. 20c., lb. 35c.

Long Giant White. Mammoth size, will yield as much per acre as the Mangle Wurtzel beets, and is equally as desirable for stock feeding; is easily harvested as it grows partly out of ground. Oz. 8c., ¼ lb 15c., lb. 45c.

CAULIFLOWER.

Bell's Early Surehead. Very early, fine flavored and one of the surest headers grown; large compact grower. One-tenth oz. 20c., ¼ oz. 45c., oz. $1.50

Henderson's Early Snowball. A dwarf compact sort; very sure header as well as extra early, being often ready for market in June. Crops of this grow where others fail. One-tenth oz. 24c., ¼ oz. 60c., oz. $1.75

CELERY.

Improved Golden Self Blanching. Pronounced by all the best early sort in cultivation. Unlike other self-blanching sorts this is a perfect keeper, fully equally in this respect some sorts whose only merits are good keeping qualities. It is entirely self blanching without any banking or covering except to bring the earth slightly around it. With this little care it assumes a light yellow or almost white appearance, with a beautiful crisp yellow heart. The stalks grow vigorously with large, thickly set ribs of handsome and uniform size. Very robust grower of unequalled appearance in the market or on the table. ¼ oz. 8c., ½ oz 15c., oz., 25c., ¼ lb. 80c.

Improved Giant Pascal. Larger than the preceding, being an extra large sort for late planting of a fine nutty flavor and free from all bitter taste; grows about two feet high, broad, thick and crisp, bleaches easily and in four to five days has a golden yellow heart, as a keeper is unexcelled. ½ oz. 10c., oz. 18c., ¼ lb. 60c.

Improved White Plume. A popular self-blanching sort, early, crisp and of a rich flavor. ½ oz. 8c., oz. 15c., ¼ lb. 40c.

IMPROVED LONG ORANGE.

BELL'S PROLIFIC PICKLING.

CUCUMBER.

Early Cluster. Very early and productive; grows in clusters. Oz. 8c, ¼ lb. 18c, lb. 50c.

New Everbearing. Extra early and continues to bear fruit in great abundance the entire season whether the ripe fruit is picked or not. Remarkably solid, with few seeds and of fine quality for slicing or pickling. ⅛ oz. 7c. oz. 12c, ¼ lb. 20c, lb. 80c.

Bell's Prolific Pickling. The best and most productive pickling sort grown; fair size, uniform shape and superior quality; immensely productive. ½ oz. 6c, oz. 10c, ¼ lb. 25c, lb. 75c.

White Wonder. Surpasses any other White Cucumber in handsome appearance and fine quality; more hardy and vigorous than other sorts and always produces large crops of perfect fruit, averaging 8 inches long and 2 inches in diameter with thin, tough, pearly white skin and brittle; exquisite quality. Pkt. 5c, ½ oz. 8c· oz. 15c, ¼ lb. 35c. lb. $1.25.

Improved Long Green. A long, firm, dark green sort, of crisp fine quality. The most popular for general culture. Oz. 8c, ¼ lb. 15c, lb. 50c.

SWEET or SUGAR CORN.

Extra Early. The earliest Corn in cultivation; fine quality, sweet; ears fair sized for so early. ½ pt. 12c, qt. 35c. Peck by express, 90c.

Medium Early. This variety follows the preceeding, being 10 to 15 days later and of larger size, it keeps in good condition till the evergreen is ready; with the three sorts you can have corn from mid-summer till frosts; exquisitely sweet and produces two to three good sized ears on each stalk. ½ pt. 12c, quart 35c, peck by express 90c.

Stowell's Evergreen. The old standard late sort; mammoth size and fine quality. The best late in every respect. ½ pt. 10c, qt. 30c.

Country Gentleman (Improved Shoe Peg.) The ears are of good size and produced in great abundance, stalks often bearing four good ears, while the average of the crop is three ears to a stalk. The cob is very small, giving great depth to the kernels, which are of pearly whiteness. One of the sweetest and most tender of all Sweet Corn. ½ pt. 14c, qt. 40c.

Borecole, or Kale. Improved Dwarf green. Dwarf and nicely curled, hardy and may be cut from ground all the early part of winter. Oz. 10c, ¼ lb. 35c.

Brussels Sprouts. Delicious little side heads; resembles small cabbages. Oz. 10c, ¼ lb. 25c.

Cress or Peppergrass. Fine Curled. Best sort for general use. Oz. 7c, ¼ lb. 15c

Water Cress. Delicious salad; grows along streams. ¼ oz. 10c.

Collards. New Georgia. Loose open heads, very popular in south. Oz. 9c.

Chicory, Large Rooted or Coffee. Used as a substitute for coffee. Oz. 15c.

Egg Plant, Early Long Purple. Early, hardy, productive. ½ oz. 10c, oz. 18c.

New York Improved. Large, round and excellent quality. Most popular sort. ½ oz. 20c, oz 35c.

Kohl Rabi, Early White Vienna. One of the best for market or table use. ½ oz. 10c, oz. 18c, ¼ lb. 60c

White Mustard. Preferred for salads or culinary purposes. Oz. 7c, ¼ lb. 15c.

KOHL RABI.

LETTUCE

FERRY'S EARLY PRIZE HEAD.

Ferry's Early Prize-Head, Mammoth plants, leaves crisp, slow to run up to seed, hardy, excellent flavor and lasts well. Oz. 9c, ¼ lb. 35c, lb. $1.30

Tomhannock. An entirely distinct lettuce of extra fine quality; forms a large and beautiful plant, leaves grow upright with upper part turning out; the leaves within are almost white and are wonderfully crisp and tender; grows quickly and is slow to run up seed. ¼ oz. 10c, oz. 18 ¼ lb. 50c.

Grand Rapids Forcing. Splendid and profitable forcing lettuce. Where the lettuce is cultivated in greenhouses the entire yield often averages from one to two pounds each, and three crops may be taken from the ground each season, if the soil be made very rich. Readily sells for a higher price than ordinary sorts, and is one of the best for shipping. ½ oz. 8c, oz. 18c, ¼ lb. 50c.

Improved Defiance Summer, It produces a splendid, large, solid head of the cabbage type, remaining a long time in prime condition without going to seed. It is of a light green color, fine quality, crisp and tender,

HANSON LETTUCE.

and in rich soil, well watered if it does not rain often nearly every plant will perfect a fine solid head in the hottest summer weather, when some other varieties will even refuse to grow. ½ oz 9c, oz, 15c, ¼ lb. 40c.

Hanson, This is a favorite with many people. Heads are large and of excellent quality. It grows quickly and will stand the summer well. Oz. 9c, ¼lb. 32c, lb. $1 20.

Denver Market, This novelty in Lettuce forms beautiful large solid heads of a delicate light green color; the leaves are blistered like a Savoy cabbage. Tender, of excellent quality, is good to sow early in the ground. Pkt. 5c, oz. 20c, ¼ lb. 50c.

NEW NETTED BEAUTY MELON.

This is one of the earliest and best melons grown. Although not so large as some the enormous number produced make it a profitable sort to grow, but when we consider that the Melons bring double the prices of other sorts it makes it doubly so. Each vine produces 8 to 10 perfect, thick fleshed Melons of the richest and most luscious flavor. Large packet 6c, 2 pkts 10c, ½ oz 12c, oz. 20c, ¼lb. 65c, lb $1.75

Extra Early Prolific Nutmeg, This is the earliest of all. The flavor is extra rich and luscious; they grow to a fair size and are produced in great number. Oz 9c, ¼ lb 20c, lb. 70c.

Emerald Gem, Deep emerald green, thin rind; flesh suffused salmon color, unequalled in its rich, delicious flavor, vines thrifty and prolific. We urge all to try this variety. ½oz. 8c, oz. 12c, ¼lb. 30c, lb. 9½c.

The Banquet. A beautiful netted, medium sized, red fleshed sort of a granular melting quality which is unsurpassed. It will produce as many if not more edible melons to the acre than any other sort. If you wish melons of the best quality, plant the Banquet. Large packet 5c, ½oz. 12c, oz. 20c, ¼lb 60c, lb. $1 50.

Bell's Improved Casaba. A large sized melon of the most delicious flavor. Has proved to be one of the surest croppers, thick and solid. Will, under cultivation, average 15 lbs. each. Oz.10c, ¼lb. 25c, lb. 90c.

The Princess. Handsome appearance, heavy netted, dark green skin. The flesh is of rich salmon color, and thicker than in any other melon. The flavor is sweet and luscious. They ripen early, and grow to good size, averaging 8 to 10 pounds. Vines grow vigorously, are very productive, often 7 or 8 perfect melons on a vine. Pkt. 6c, 2 pkts. 10c, oz. 12c, ¼lb. 35c, lb. $1.00.

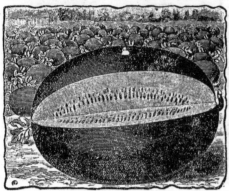

HENDERSON'S GREEN AND GOLD.

WATER MELON.

Bell's Improved Early. Best for an extra early sort, and will succeed farther north than most varieties. Fair size and rich, sweet, melting flavor. Oz. 8c., ¼ lb. 20c., lb. 65c.

Bell's Shipper. Large size, solid, very prolific, producing immense crops and bears shipping well. This is a profitable sort to grow. Oz. 8c., ¼ lb. 20c, lb. 65c.

Dixie. Handsome fresh appearance, and fine quality, remarkably thin rind, almost unpenetratable which preserves it for a great length of time before showing decay. Each vine will mature from six to eight large perfect melons, of luscious flavor; color is a dark green with beautiful stripes. Oz. 9c., ¼ lb. 20c., lb. 60c.

Henderson's Green and Gold. The largest and most deliciously flavored of the early melons. Weight ranges from 25 to 40 pounds. Rind is thinest of all; flesh a beautiful golden orange, extremely sweet and juicy. Oz. 8c., ¼ lb. 18c., lb. 50c. See cut.

NEW EXTRA EARLY PEARL ONION.

ONION.

Extra Early Pearl. This remarkable onion is among the earliest and best of all white varieties. It grows to enormous size and shape as shown in the illustration; of pearly white color, the outer skin having a most snowy wax appearance, flesh of a pure snowy white, and flavor so mild that it can be eaten like an apple. It grows with a wonderful rapidity, reaching the first season an enormous size. A splendid keeper, succeeding everywhere and requiring only thin soil. Pkt. 6c., 2 pkts. 10c., ½ oz. 18c., oz. 35c.; ¼ lb. $1.35, lb. $4.50.

Extra Early White Pickling. Very early, silvery white, flesh firm and mild, for pickling it is unequalled. ½ oz. 10c., oz. 18c., ¼ lb. 65c.

Extra Early Red. Medium size, flat variety; abundant producer and of uniform size and shape; desirable for early market, being about two weeks ear-

lier than Red Wethersfield. ½ oz. 8c., oz. 15c., ¼ lb. 45c., lb. $1.45.

Spanish King, or Prizetaker. Pronounced the largest, handsomest and most profitable onion to grow; rich yellow color outside with pure, white, mild, sweet and tender flesh, can be eaten raw like an apple. Often grows 7 inches in diameter, and weighs three to four lbs. As high as 1,127 bushels have been grown on one acre. They always bring a big price in any market.

1 pkt. 6c., 2 pkts. 10c., ½ oz. 12c., oz. 20c., ¼ lb. 70c., lb. $2.50.

Mammoth Silver King. One of the largest onions ever grown, often weighing from two to four lbs., and being from fifteen to twenty inches in circumference. Skin is a silvery white, flesh snow white flavor mild and pleasant. can be eaten raw, matures early. ½ oz. 10c., oz. 20c., ¼ lb. 75c., lb. $2.75.

Giant Rocco. Mild, delicate flavor, immense size, globular shape, and a very good keeper. Oz. 15c., ¼ lb. 50c., lb. $1.60.

SPANISH KING.

3¾ LBS

ONIONS,
concluded.

Selected Yellow Globe Danvers. A finely formed strain of this remarkable and popular onion, with flavor just suited to general use. This is the most popular onion grown, always producing a good crop keeping well and salable in any market. Seeds grown from selected bulbs. Oz. 10c., ¼ lb. 35c., lb. $1.25, 5 lbs. or over, by express, $1.00 per lb.

Large Red Wethersfield. Large size, with a deep purplish red skin; flesh almost white, fine grained and rather strong flavor. Very productive, good keeper and popular for general market, especially in the west. Oz. 10c., ¼ lb. 35c., lb. $1.25, 5 lbs or over, by express, $1.00 per lb.

Giant Red Globe. Mild, mammoth sized onion succeeding almost everywhere and producing a large crop of splendid globe-shaped bulbs which always command a high price. ½ oz. 8c, oz. 15c, ¼ lb. 55c., lb. $2.00.

YELLOW GLOBE DANVERS.

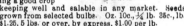

PEAS.

☞ All Northern grown, hand picked and of the finest possible quality.

Bell's Extra Early. Two and one-half feet high, round, good cropper, very early. An improvement on First and Best and Extra Early. ½ pt. 12c., 1 pt. 20c., 1 qt. 35c. By express $1.00 per peck, $3.75 per bush.

Bell's Second Early. 18 inches high, wrinkled, best early for market gardeners and general home crop; stands without support. ½ pt. 12c., 1 qt. 35c. By express $1.00 per peck, $3.75 per bush.

Bell's Medium Early. Immense yielder, about two feet high, stocky and branching, does not need bushing, large and sweet. ½ pt. 12c., 1 pt. 20c., 1 qt. 40c. By express $1.10 per peck, $4.00 per bush.

BELL'S SECOND EARLY PEA.

Champion of England. Sweet, grows tall, immensely productive considered the best all-round late wrinkled pea. ½ pt. 10c., pt. 18c, 1 qt. 32c. By express 85c per peck, $2.75 per bush.

Marrowfats. Best sort for field sowing with oats, etc.; great bearers, pods large and full. ½ pt. 10c, 1 qt. 30c. By express 65c. pk., $2 bu

☞ Remember, if you order by express or freight, you paying express or freight charges when you receive the seeds, you can deduct 16c. from price of a quart or 4c. from price of a ½ pint, or 8c. from price of a pound. This is the amount we pay for postage on seeds. On a large order you can save by doing this unless you are a great distance from us.

BELL'S MEDIUM EARLY PEA.

PARSNIPS.

Long Hollow Crown. Smooth, well-formed roots, the best for table use or stock. Oz. 7c , ¼ lb. 15c., lb. 45c.

Improved Guernsey. A greatly improved and fine strain of Guernsey. The roots do not grow so long as the Hollow Crown, but larger in diameter and are more easily gathered; a very heavy cropper. Roots smooth, flesh fine grained and of excellent quality. Strictly a table variety. Oz. 8c., ¼ lb. 20c., lb. 50c.

Long Smooth White. Roots long, white, sweet, smooth and tender; hardy and keeps well. Oz. 7c., ¼ lb. 15c., lb. 45c.

PROCOPP'S GIANT PEPPER.

PEPPER.

1045—Mammoth Ruby King, The plants are crowded full of large, handsome and bright ruby-red peppers, which have such a mild and delicate flavor that they make a pleasant and appetizing salad. The fruit is from six to eight inches, and four inches through. Plants are strong and vigorous. ¼oz. 10c, ½oz. 18c, oz. 35c.

1044—Mammoth Golden Queen, The average specimen is handsome in shape, and of uniform size, and about twice as large as the average Golden Dawn. The Golden Queen is really a giant pepper, the fruit being from six to eight inches long, and four to five inches in diameter. Grown on rich soil, you will be able to count twelve to fifteen perfect, handsome fruits on a single plant, all of a bright, waxy golden color, and of an extremely mild and delicious flavor. Will sell in any market for double the price of other varieties. ¼oz. 12c, ½oz. 20c, oz. 35c.

1044—Procopp's Giant Pepper, This variety may justly be called the Goliath of all the Pepper family. They grow uniformly to a very large size The shape is well depicted in our illustration. They are of a brilliant scarlet color, flesh fully one-half inch in thickness, in flavor they are just hot enough to be pleasant to the taste. Each plant ripens from eight to twelve perfect handsome fruits, eight to ten inches long, by three inches thick. ½ oz. 15c, oz. 35c, 2 oz. 65c, ¼ lb. $1.25.

PUMPKIN.

Early Pie, Very productive, ripens early, of medium size ; exceedingly fine flavored when cooked ; rich colored and very fine grained. very dry and sweet. Oz. 10c, ¼ lb. 25c, lb. 80c.

Northern Giant, This mammoth Pumpkin is of such colossal size and fine appearance that it is sure to win the premium wherever exhibited. Often weighs 200 to 300 lbs. ; is fine grained, sweet and dry. Pkt. 5c, oz. 12c, ¼ lb. 30c, lb. $1.00.

Field Crop. Very productive and the best for field crop or planting with corn. Oz. 6c, ¼ lb. 12c, lb. 35c.

SQUASH.

Early Summer Crookneck, This is an improved strain of the popular Crookneck and is the best summer squash. Oz. 8c, ¼ lb. 18c, lb. 50c.

Fordhook, Earliest winter Squash ; keeps long, fine flavor, dry and sweet. Oz. 10c, ¼ lb. 25c, lb. 80c.

Faxon, Flesh deep orange ; enormously productive, is early, of extra quality and keeps long. Considered by many preferable to the Hubbard. Oz. 10c, ¼ lb. 25c, lb. 80c.

IMPROVED HUBBARD.

Improved Hubbard, This is an improved quality of standard winter Squash, very dry, sweet and unexcelled for table use, grows good size and is a splendid keeper. Oz. 8c, ¼ lb. 16c, lb. 55c.

PARSLEY.

1037—Giant Curled, Large, finely curled. A popular sort. Oz. 8c, ¼ lb. 24c, lb. 80c.

1058—New Fern Leaf, One of the best and most ornamental for table decorations. A handsome garden plant. Oz. 9c, ¼ lb. 24c.

SALSIFY OR VEGETABLE OYSTER.

1088—White French, A desirable substitute for oysters. Oz. 12c. ¼ lb. 40c.

1089—Mammoth Sandwich Island, The best variety ; has large, white, smooth roots, double the size of ordinary roots. Half oz. 10c, oz. 20c, ¼ lb. 60c.

Biz

RADISHES.

Bell's Selected Forcing, Very best extra early radish for forcing, or for early sowing. Oz. 9c, ¼ lb. 18c. 60c.

1057—Scarlet Turnip, Handsome, crisp and tender, grows quickly, fine for early. Oz. 8c, ¼ lb. 18c, lb. 50c.

1059—Long Scarlet Short Top, One of the best for general cultivation, 6 to 7 inches long, brittle and tender. Oz. 8c, ¼ lb. 18c, lb. 60c.

1064—White Strasburg, Flesh firm, brittle and tender, retains its crispness when old ; oblong and pure white. grows quickly and withstands heat. Nearly the same as the "Newcomb Radish," but superior. Oz. 8c, ¼ lb. 15c, lb. 65c.

1065—French Breakfast, Quick growth, mild and tender. Oz. 8c, ¼ lb. 18c. lb. 65c.

1067—Chinese Rose Winter, Large, firm and excellent winter radish. Oz. 9c, ¼ lb. 20c, lb. 80c.

1068—California Mammoth Winter, Pure white, excellent quality, about one foot long and 2 to 3 inches in diameter: keeps well in winter. Oz. 10c, ¼ lb. 24c. lb. 80c.

SPINACH.

Round or Summer, Early for spring growing. Oz. 6c, ¼ lb. 14c, lb. 35c.

Long Standing, Thick Leaved, One of the best of market sorts. It produces a large, thick, strong green leave somewhat crumpled, and possesses the valuable quality of standing a long time before running to seed. Oz. 7c, ¼ lb. 38c.

Prickly or Fall, Hardiest, and stands winter well. Oz. 7c, ¼ lb. 14c, lb. 40c.

POTATOES.

Our seed is choice, grown by us especially for seed purposes. **PRICE:—***By mail, 6 eyes with pieces of potato enough to make grow, 10c, 25 eyes, assorted or one sort, 25c, 100 eyes, 70c, 1lb. 10 c. By express: 10c. lb., peck 60c. bushel $1.50.*

New Prolific Bug-Proof Potato, Hardiest and most productive variety in this section always producing a good crop, even in an unfavorable season. Potatoes good size, fine form, rather elongated, excellent keeper. Bugs do not harm tops.

New Columbia Beauty Potato, Skin white, flesh pure white, dry, mealy, and of the best possible quality. Extra early and a good keeper. Large producer.

Stray Beauty, Extremely early ; when the size of walnuts, are dry and mealy. Round form, rose color.

Rural New Yorker No. 2, One of the best ; handsome appearance ; large size with remarkable smoothness of skin ; extreme whiteness of skin and flesh.

TOMATO.

Bell's Extra Early Improved, The earliest in cultivation, good size, smooth and of excellent flavor; is equally as early as the small rough tomatoes sold for extra early; often ripe in June; rich red color. Pkt. 6c, 2 pkt. 10c, ½ oz. 15c, oz. 25c, ¼lb. 80c.

Bell's Medium, A fine size, uniform, solid. beautiful tomato following the extra early and ripening up an immense crop in good season for use. In color, productiveness, flavor and solidity it is unsurpassed. Try it once and you will want no other. Pkt. 6c, 2 pkt. 10c, ½oz. 15c, oz. 25c, ¼ lb. 80c.

Bell's Mammoth Late, Very late, immensely productive, solid, heavy, vigorous grower, ripens later than the medium, but produces rather more. Pkt. 6c, 2 pkts. 10c, ½oz. 15c, ¼ lb. 85c.

Livingston's Beauty. The crowning one of Mr. Livingston's great tomatoes; enormous yielder, grows in clusters, late, extra shipper. ½oz. 10c, oz. 20c, ¼ lb. 70c.

Strawberry or Winter Cherry, Grows enclosed in a husk and will keep within the husks all winter; very sweet flavored, small yellow fruits; excellent for preserves, for which alone it is worth while raising; immensely productive, and fine quality. It is very much earlier and every way better than a similar variety advertised as a novelty under name of Cape Gooseberry, while it is incomparably better than the "Improved Ground Cherry." It has a strawberry flavor, which gives it a relish to eat out of hand. Dried in sugar as raisins or figs, or for use in fruit cakes, it is unexcelled. ½oz. 15c, oz. 25c.

TURNIPS.

1122—Extra Early Purple Top Munich, The earliest of all. Oz. 8c, ¼ lb. 18c, lb. 50c.

1120—Strap Leaf Purple Top. The most popular variety for table use; is fine grained and rich. Oz. 8c, ¼ lb. 15c, lb. 45c; 5 lbs. or over by express 80c. per lb.

STRAP LEAF PURPLE TOP.

1126—White Sweet, (Ruta-Baga. Excellent for table and stock, solid and keeps well. Oz. 8c, ¼ lb. 15c, lb. 50c.

1127—Carter's Imperial Purple Top, (Ruta-Baga.) One of the best purple top sorts for table or stock; flesh yellow, firm and sweet and yields heavily. Oz. 8c, ¼lb. 18c, lb. 50c.

The price of all our Vegetable Seeds (except a few higher priced ones where the price is given) is 4c. per packet, or if you order 10 or more packets, 3c. a packet; they contain about the same quantity as ordinary 5c. pkts. We guarantee them fresh and reliable.

RHUBARB.

Bell's Giant Victoria, Medium early, mammoth size, fine quality, the best sort for family use. ½ oz 9c, oz. 15c.

HERBS.

This list comprises the most desirable varieties for seasoning soups, meats, etc., and for medicinal purposes. Cut when dry before they blossom, dry in the shade and pack in a tight box. *Any variety 3 cts. a packet; six or more packets at 2½ cts. each.*

Name.	Use	Oz.
Anise	Garnishes and sea's'ng.	15c
Balm	Balm tea and wine	20
Basil, Sweet	Seasoning soups	20
Caraway	Confectionery	8
Catnip	Medical	40
Coriander	Garnishes, etc.	8
Dill	Soups and Pickles	9
Hoarhound	Cough medicine	24
Hyssop	Hyssop tea	15
Lavender	Aromatic, Medical	10
Marjoram, Sweet	Seasoning	15
Rosemary	Aromatic seas'ng	50
Rue	Croup in fowls, medic'n'l	20
Saffron	Medicinal, etc.	15
Sage	Seasoning, dressing	10
Sweet Fennell, Aromatic		10
Summer Savory	Flavoring	10
Thyme	Seasoning, headache	30
Wormwood	Medicinal	30

VINE PEACH.

2000—The fruit is about the size of a large peach, oval shaped, and of a bright orange yellow color, somewhat russeted. When it first ripens it is quite hard and has but little flavor, but soon they become mellow and sweet and have a rich flavor. When ripe the fruit fall from the vine, the flesh is very firm with a cavity in the centre, and when peeled and the seeds taken out they much resemble peaches. For sweet pickles, pies or preserving they are superb. Where fruit is scarce, we feel certain that they will quickly become popular, as they are easily cultivated, wonderfully prolific and can be used in every way in which you would use a peach, except that they are not usually liked raw, although some consider them excellent simply sliced with a little sugar on. Market gardners are already having considerable call for them from their customers. The vine on which they are borne is somewhat similar to the muskmelon vine, and requires the same cultivation. Pkt. 6c, 2 pkts. 10c, ½oz. 20c, oz. 35c.

SELECTED *FLOWER* SEEDS.

OUR List of Flower Seeds includes nearly every sort which can successfully be grown from seeds, and is of real merit. We have omitted hundreds of sorts which may be called pretty and yet are far inferior to similar varieties in this List. Our Mixtures contain the finest and best assortment of colors possible to produce, and the prices are far below what flower seeds of similar high quality are usually sold for. Each variety is preceded by a number, and in ordering you can just as well mark the number as to write the name.

Special Discount on Flower Seeds in packets only. For 50 cts. you may select 60 cts. worth of Flower Seeds; for $1.00 you may select $1.25 worth of Flower Seeds in packets. Orders over one dollar's worth 25 per cent. (or ¼) discount from the list prices.

ANNUAL PLANTS.

The seeds of the following plants may be sown in the spring, either started in the house or open ground, and they will grow and blossom in the open ground.

1. **Abronia.** Mixed colors; beautiful trailing plant, with Verbena-like flowers, colors yellow and lilac. Pkt. of seeds, 3c.

14. **Adonis.** Show mixed; very pretty showy plants for beds or borders; bright scarlet and red flowers. Pkt. 3c.

23. **Agrostemma.** "Rose of Heaven," very pretty pink-like blossoms, pkt. 3c

40. **Ambrosia.** Long stems of spray-like foliage. Pkt. 5c.

21. **Ageratum.** Show Mixed, pretty little plants remaining in bloom a long time and often blossoming well in the winter if removed to house before cold weather. Pkt. 3c.

49. **Antirrhinun or Snap-dragon.** Show mixed; brilliant and beautiful, blooms first season from seed, lives several years. Pkt. 4c

122. **Brachycome.** "Swan River Daisy," about 1 ft. high, fine in masses, brilliant white and blue flowers. Pkt. 4c.

116. **Beta.** Foliage Beet; large ornamental leaves, very nice specimen plants. Pkt, 3c.

136. **Calendula.** Meteor; large double flowers, orange and white, beautifully imbricated. Pkt. 3c.

138. **Calendula.** Double White; fine large distinct white Pkt. 4c.

41. **Calliopsis.** Golden Wave; the best yellow flower grown for cut flowers or masses, blossoms 1 to 3 inch. in diameter freely produced. Pkt. 4c.

39. **Amaranthus.** Show mixed, pretty foliage plants including a great many varieties, such as Fountain Plant, Love lies Bleeding, Princess Feather, Sunrise, etc., differing widely in habits but all very pretty. Pkt. 4c.

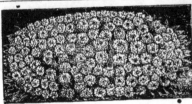

27. **Sweet Allysum.** Beautiful spreading plants with long spikes of sweet-scented white blossoms; blooms freely the entire season; it is one of the best of white flowers for cuttings or bouquets; blooms in the winter if removed to the house. Pkt. 4c. See cut.

154. **Candytuft.** Snow Queen distinct and spreading, makes beautiful masses of white, or fine for cut flowers. (See cut showing one plant.) Pkt. 4c

160. **Candytuft.** Mixed; best sort in all colors mixed, indispensible for cutting. pkt. 3

153. **Candytuft.** New Empress. This is a giant form of the Rocket Candytuft, producing trusses of white blossoms 4-8 in. long, resembling Hyacinths. Pkt. 5c.

ASTERS.

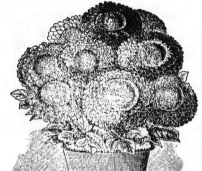

BELL'S WINDSOR BEAUTY ASTER.

ROSE FLOWERED ASTER.

Per Pkt

55 **Harlequin**—Oddly, beautifully striped, double	07
56 **Peachblossom**—Large double flowers, fine tint	08
57 **Corcardeau or Crown**—Showy double blossoms	07
58 **Fire Demon**—Lovely pompone-flowered, scarlet	07
59 **Goliath**—Mammoth, beautiful mixed colors	06
61 **Mount Blanc**—Large white blossoms, desirable	06
62 **Pæony Flowered**—Perfect pæony shape, lovely	05
64 **Rose Flowered**—Large double like a rose, mixed	05
66 **Washington**—One of the largest. 4 to 5 in. across	08
68 **Comet**—Novel, like a Chrysanthemum, double	10
74 **Queen of Halls**—Early flowering, long stems	06
75 **Victoria**—Handsomest large sort of delicate color	06
76 **Black Shakespeare**—Almost black, rather small	07
77 **Mixed Dwarf Bouquet**—Small, compact, 6–8 in. high, 14 choice mixed colors, like a bouquet	06
78 **Dwarf Chrysanthemum**—Six in. high, very rich	07
81 **Bell's Show Mixed**—Mixture of all the rarest	05
82 **Bell's Apple Blossom**—Free blooming, symmetrical. large flowers, delicate apple blossom	10
84 **Yellow Victoria**—Strong grower, rare yellow	10
85 **Windsor Beauty**—Free blooming dwarf, outer petals one color, the inner another shade	10
86 **Scarlet Triumph**—Most beautiful of the dwarf	10
87 **New Mosaic**—Free bloomer, blossoms mosaic-like	10
65—**Jewel or Ball**—Apple blossom color, blossoms round or ball-shaped, 9 in. in circumference..................	10
8,000 **Vick's New White Branching**—Blossoms just before the Chrysanthemums, and resembles them so closely as to be often sold for them................................	15
3,001 **Snowball**—Best white for bouquets, etc.................	10
3,004 **Indigo King**—Indigo on white ground, novel..............	10

BALSAM.

94 **Alabaster or Daisy Miller.**—Perfect Camellia Flowers of immense size, often 3 in. across, pure white with lavander shade, deep in flower; blossoms almost smother the foliage. pkt. 6c; 2 pkts. 10c.

95 **Bell's Defiance Striped.**—Grand strain of new colors, beautifully striped and spotted, double as roses. One of the best mixtures of Balsams ever offered. pkt 6c; 2 pkt 10c.

100 **Show Mixed.**—Grand assortment rare double sorts. pkt. 5c.

163 **Canna**, Show Mixed. Grand stately plants, fine lawn specimens. 4 to 6 ft. high. pkt. 4c.

169 **Canna**, Crozys or Gladiolus; Magnificent strain of large free flowering Cannas. Flowers as freely as gladiolus and are more brilliant: colors run through shades of crimson, scarlet, yellow striped, mottled, etc. Seeds sown in spring flower by July or August. Pkt. 10c.

183 **Celosia or Cockscomb.**—Curious ornametal plants with large heads of bright colors. Pkt. 4c.

You can Order by Number Preceeding Names.

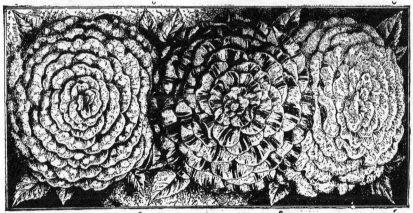

SPECIMEN BLOSSOMS OF BELL'S DEFIANCE STRIPED BALSAM.

...uria, Show mixed, ...e selection of rare new sorts of Bachelor's Button Sweet Sultan, Corn Flower, very much prettier than the old sorts; pkt....................4c

208—Clarkia, Show mixed; pretty annuals, free bloomers, double and single; pkt......3c

201—Chrysanthemum, Annual varieties mixed; free bloomers, very showy for summer flowering plants, large as the Asters; pkt 4c

245—Dwarf Morning Glory, or Convolvulus Minor, mixed; showy, brilliant plants, 1 to 2 feet high, covered with bloom at mid-day; pkt 3c

DAHLIA, ROSALIND MIXT.

244—Cosmos, rapid-growing bushy plants, 4–5 feet high, foliage pretty and completely covered with flowers the latter part of the season; pkt 3

258—Dahlia, Rosalind mixture; only the rare new sorts of great beauty; pkt.......................15c

262—Dahlia, Double mixed; seeds sown early produce good flowering plants by autumn and are usually more satisfactory than bulbs; grand plants for autumn blooming; pkt..................................10c

265—Daisy, Double mixed; pretty perennials, bloom first season from seed, fine for borders and blooms from spring until the frosts come; pkt...............5c

424—Mimulus, Show mixed; brilliant blossoms richly colored and spotted and marked making the plants of indescribable beauty; pkt 8c

478—Evening Primrose, New Mexican; dwarf and trailing plants covered with bright rose blossoms, 5c

468—Nicotiana, Show mixed; very choice assortment of these grand flowers; many are two inches long and pure waxy white; pkt.........................5c

607—Pyrethrum, hardy in this section and blooms abundantly; is almost as desirable as an Aster; pkt. 4c

619—Salpiglossis, Show mixed; showy bedding or border plants, with richly colored, erect, funnel-shaped flowers; the colors are beautifully marbled and penciled, purple, scarlet, crimson, buff, blue and almost black; pkt...................................4c

267—Datura, double mixed, called "Angels' Trumpet," large branching plant with trumpet-shaped, fragrant blossoms, equal in beauty to many of our lilies; pkt 4c

310—Eschscholtzia, Show mixed; known as California Poppy; foliage beautifully cut, blossoms brilliant and freely produced; pkt 3c

312—Four-o'clock, Show mixed; also called Marvel of Peru, and Mirabilis; well known and pretty plants; pkt. 3c, oz. 10c.

700—Euphorbia, Heterophylla; resembles the flaming scarlet leaves of the Poinsettia; this rare plant grows readily from seeds; pkt.............10c

GODETIA.

321—Gaillardia, Show mixed, very gay colored blossoms abundantly produced from July till fall; fine for masses or cut flowers; pkt...............3c

337—Godetia, Show mixed; blossoms rich and satin-like, their richness always attracts much attention; finest sorts only; pkt..................4c

401—Lobelia, Show mixed; a charming genus of dwarf plants suited to edgings, rock-work, hanging baskets, etc.; drooping foliage and blue and white blossoms; pkt..................................4c

391—Larkspur, Show mixed; pretty spikes of bloom, fine for bouquets, etc; some almost resemble Hyacinths; pkt..............................3c

409—Mesembryanthemum, Mixed; fine for hanging baskets, etc., called Ice Plant; pkt...........3c

419—Mignonette, Show mixed; sweet scented; all the large flowering varieties; pkt............4c

8040—Ricinus, Zanzibariensis; grand stately plants with handsome colored foliage more beautiful than palms and make large plants from seed early in the season; some are 8 to 10 feet high; this is much improved strain of Ricinus; pkt. 6c, 2 for 10c

625—Scabiosa, Pretty showy plants, double and of all conceivable colors; blossoms very freely produced; pkt...................................4c

546—Portulacca, Single mixed; rich and dazzling brilliancy completely hiding foliage; pkt................3c

546½—Portulacca, Double mixed; all richest colors; forms a carpet of bloom, plants mostly come double; pkt. 8c

630—Butterfly Flower, Fragrant and free blooming annuals of much interest and beauty; resembles the markings of orchids; flowers pure white and double, and the petals cut in a picturesque manner; pkt..................4c

630—Sensitive Plant, A curious plant; will close and droop at the slightest touch;..................4c

Bell's
Gorgeous Nasturtiums.

For years our Nasturtiums have been the admiration of everybody for their brilliancy and free flowering characteristics. They are among the most satisfactory plants, always producing an abundance of richly colored bloom, every color and combination of color

DWARF OR TOM THUMB NASTURTIUM.

487—Empress of India, New dark, leaved variety...4c
488—Crimson...3c
439—Rose, Soft rose..............................3c
440—Yellow...3c
441—Spotted, Beautiful.............................3c
442—Beauty, Canary and scarlet............... 3c
443—Scarlet, Flashing scarlet..................3c
444—Crystal Palace Gem, Sulphur and maroon....3c
448—Coerluco Roseum, Beautiful peach color....3c
449—Bronze King, A rich crimson bronze.......4c
452—White Pearl, A very fine white sort..... ..5c
454—Tom Thumb, Dwarf Mixed, (Oz. 20c.) 3c

One packet each above sorts dwarf Nasturtiums, 35 cents.

CLIMBING NASTURTIUMS.

455—Purple and Gold, Golden yellow cc
456—Dunnett's Orange, Dark orange.......34
457—Edward Otto, Silky bronze...........3c
458—Pearl, Very delicate white...........4c
459—Coccineum, Scarlet..................3c
46c—Striped Varieties, Assorted varieties ..3c
461—Regelianum, Violet crimson...........3c
462—Schillingii, Bright yellow............2c
701—Von Moltke, Beautiful rose...... .....3c
728—Brown King, Showy brown......; ..3c
463—Mixed, All colors (oz. 15cts.)..........2c

One packet each variety of above Climbing Nasturtiums, 25c.

GAY DIANTHUS PINKS.

276—Mourning Cloak, nearly black, handsome 5c
278—Heddewigii, large, double, brilliant colors.....5c
279—Japanese Pink, Striped and fringed...........5c
280—The Bride or Little Gem, dwarf, magnificent..5c
281—Laciniatus, rich in hue, very double 6c
282—Diadematus, densely double, rich hue.........4c
283—Eastern Queen, Large double flowers. stained 4c
284—Double Yellow, choice novel color 4c
285—Snowflake, large white flowers, fringed 4c
286—Imperialis, fl. pl, superb double variety, ...4c
289—New Cyclops, very novel, robust. fragrant....10c
291—Double White, large, pure white, double 3c
294—Bell's Show Mixed, selection of finest sorts ..4c

SHOWY POPPIES.

514—New Shirley, flowers large, graceful, elegant 4
515—Double Carnation Flowered, very elegant.. 3
516—Mikado, charming double striped, fringed, 4
517—Peacock, brilliant scarlet, glossy black ring, 4
518—Iceland Poppy, hardy perennials, brilliant 4
520—Riverdale Mixture, choice showy mixture 3
523—Double Pompone, dwarf double, varied......4
524—Spotted Beauty, deep scarlet, white spots..4
525—Striped Beauty, white ground, red stripes..5
526—Chamois Rose, new, large ball shaped......4
527—New Oriental, a new hybrid, very elegant 4
529 –Fairy Blush, finest of all, very large, rich..5
530—Snowdrift, Snow white, very double, choice 5

Gorgeous Petunias.
Extremely showy, producing showy blossoms from June till cut down by the frosts; for bedding purposes they have few equals.

781—Finest Striped and Blotched, beautifully veined, 4
889—Bell's Inimitable, large flowering; blossoms large and distinct, finest mixt. for house flowering......10

782—Show Mixture, all choicest single varieties 4
778—Bell's Double Mixed, choice selected d'ble 10
776—California Giant—Mammoth single mixed 15

PHLOX Drummondii.

For a splendid mass of brilliant colors and constant display, this is unexcelled; commences to bloom early in summer, and it produces gay flowers in lavish abundance till frosts come.

549—Cuspidata, or Star of Quedlinburgh Central teeth 5 to 6 times as long as lateral ones, great oddity, star-shaped. pk 10
550—Brilliant Scarlet, very rich, pkt 5c
556—Double White Blossoms large and double. pkt 10c
555--Dwarf Mammoth, dwarf, flowers large, all desirable colors, pkt ... s... 10
560 - Stellata, dazzling, with white center, blooms freely. 6c
562—Palisade Mixture, The grandest mixture of Phlox ever offered, all rare and new sorts, 1 kt 8c
564---Fine Mixed, All varieties, ½ oz. 20c pkt.................4c

☞ One pkt. each of 16 choice sorts for 75c.

PHLOX, PALISADE MIXTURE.

Lordly VERBENAS.

One of the most eagerly sought for plants in cultivation Plants raised from seed are better than those from cuttings.
663 Lemon, The delightful fragrance of its leaves makes this variety indispensble in bouquets pkt 8c
665 Dwarf Hybrida, Dwarf and compact, four elegant colors, pkt, 15c
666 Large Flowered, known as the Mammoth Verbena Vigorous grower, 8c
669 Show Mixed Seeds saved only from choice specimens, of rich color and good size....8c
670 Finest Scarlet. Blossoms intensely scarlet......8c
664 New Golden Leaved. Intense blossoms contrasting finely with the golden yellow foliage, effective, ..15c
673 Finest Mixed, all the choice varieties.... ....5c

STOCK--Gilly Flower.

640—Ten Weeks Stock, Mixed Colors. Very choice selections; double, very rare strains...............8c
641—Perpetual Flowering, Extremely free-flowering; has fine habits........... 10
644—New, White Perfection, valuable for cutting.10
645—Blood Red Bouquet, very choice............10

ZINNIAS.

794—New Pompon, Mixed colors.................5c
793—Selected Dwarf, Extra fine strains [See cut.]4c
795—Zebra, Finely striped blossoms..............5c
796—Mammoth, Extra large, very double........4c
797—Double Mixed, All choice colors...........8c
1316—New zinnia, Curled and Crested: A rare class; very double and curled......................8c

Seeds of these sown in the open ground in Spring or Early Summer make plants which will flower the next season and live year after year in the open ground.

91. **Auricula.**—Bell's Show Mixed. A great favorite in Europe; bears great umbels of beautiful fragrant flowers: it is a species of Primrose. Per pkt. 5c.

237 **Commelina**—Profuse and splendid bloomer, blooms 1st season. Pkt. 4c.

170 **Canterbury Bell** Double mixed; very popular biennial produces an abundance ricely colored bloom. Pkt. 3c.

235 **Columbine**—Queen Victoria Mixed. Rare new sorts, mostly double; these are among our most showy hardy plants. Pkt. 6c., two pkts. 10c.

8 **Achillea**—Double White; one of the finest free-blooming hardy plants for cemetery planting, loaded with hundreds of double white blossoms at a time. Packet 10c.

15 **Adonis**—Vernalis; strong large flowers, fine for clumps. Pkt 3c

30 **Allysum**—Saxatile; called Gold Dust, plants compact and covered with beautiful golden yellow flowers; fine for massing or rock work. Pkt. 3c.

46 **Anemone**—One of the most brilliant of spring flowering bulbs, all rich colors represented; seed sown in the spring makes bulbs which will bloom in the winter. Pkt. 4c.

51 **Arabis**—One of the earliest and prettiest of spring flowers with neat spreading tufts. covered with pure white-flowers; always looks neat and pretty. Pkt. 4c

44 **Alpine Aster**—Or Star of Switzerland—7-9 in. high, compact, Daisy.like flowers 2 in. across, violet or sky-blue with yellow center. Pkt. 5c.

173 **Carnation**—Double mixed; very fragrant and. beautiful, the delicate markings of most sorts are exquisite. Pkt. 5c.

161 **Candytuft**—Evergreen or Sempervirens; hardy, 1 ft. high, white. Pkt. 4c.

195 **Chrysanthemum**—Maximum or Great White Moon Penny Daisy; large white flowers profusely produced throughout season, splendid for cut flowers, lasting a long time in water, plants robust and bushy. Pkt. 5c.

233 **Columbine**—Chrysantha, or Golden Spurred; Strong grow ing, beautiful variety, attaining a height of 4 ft., flowers bright yellow and abundantly produced. Pkt. 5c.

3026 **Coreopsis**—Lanceolate; blooms profusely all summer, blossoms large and showy, pure yellow, looks as if floating in the air. Pkt. 5c.

272 **Delphinum**—Show mixed; long spikes of brilliant rich bloom, foliage pinnatifid, rare sorts only. Pkt. 3c.

274 **Delphinum Sulfurum**—Or New Yellow Larkspur; a lovely plant with rich sulphur yellow blossoms resembling an orchid. Pkt. 10c.

297 **Digitalis**—Show mixed; dense spikes of bloom 3-4 feet high, blossoms thimble shaped, many choice colors. Pkt 3c

298 **Dodecatheon**—Clevelandi, or Giant American Cowslip. Stems one foot high surmounted with 6-10 Cyclamen-like flowers of violet hue with yellow and black centers; an extremely desirable hardy plant for a partially shaded situation. Pkt. 10c.

349 **Hedysarum**—French Honeysuckle; produces racemes of beautiful pea-like flowers. Pkt. 3c.

387 **Ipomopsis**—Or Standing Cypress. Delicate tree-like plants, loaded with long spikes of beautiful bloom. Pkt 3c

400 **Lychnis** Show mixed Rich and showy, flowers first season if sown early. Pkt. 3c.

403 **Lychnis**—Chalcedonica or Burning Star. Intense glowing scarlet. Pkt. 3c.

375 **Hollyhock**—Show mixed; grand old hardy plant, new sorts, full and double like a rose, all rare colors. White, purple. yellow, salmon, rose or mixed; per pkt. 5c.

433 **Myostis or Forget-me-not**—Everbody loves this beautiful plant which sends up its delicate spikes of lovely flowers early in spring. Pkt. 5c.

511 **Pansies**—Show Mixed; over 100 choice sorts, per pkt. 5c. White, black, bronze, purple, stained and striped or yellow pansies, 5c. per pkt.

536 **Pentstemone**—Show mixed; fine hardy border plant, with long tubed blossoms in pinacles, very choice. Pkt. 5c.

547 **Potentilla**—Show mixed; flowers rich and magnificent. profuse bloomer. Pkt. 5c.

540 **Phlox**—Show mixed; each plant sends up several large panicles of showy flowers making a magnificent show. Pkt 5c

573 **Polyanthus Primula**—Blooms early in spring; pkt. 5c.

617 **Romneya**—Giant California Poppy; stately and beautiful, pure white half transparent petals, blossoms 4-6 in. across, yellow stamens in center, not hardy at north. Pkt. 10c.

646 **Sweet William**—Show Mixed; grand and rare sorts; pk 3c
647 "   "   Double Mixed; choice and showy, " 5c.

654 **Valerian** or Jacob's Ladder—Beautiful pinnate leaves, blue flowers. Pkt. 3c.

Large packet of all above and other Perennial Flower Seeds, mixed together, 10c.

Seeds of these should mostly be sown in pans, pots or boxes in the house, and when yet small transplanted so as to give plenty of room. Most sorts sown in the spring will bloom the following winter.

CALCEOLARIA.

CYCLAMEN.

PRIMULA.

3 **Abutilon**—Show mixed; rare assortment of the choicest of these grand free blooming house plants, called "Flowering Maple." Colors very rich and beautiful. Pkt. 10c.

93 **Azalea**—Show mixed; one of the most beautiful house shrubs; pkt. 10c

101 **Begonia**—Tuberous Rooted, mixed; finest large-flowering sorts; pkt. 10c.; bulbs, double and single mixed, fine sorts, 10c. each, 3 for 25c., 75c. per doz.

112 " Choice mixed; all fine sorts of fancy-leaved and flowering sorts 10c. per pkt.

113 " Vernon; brilliant orange carmine flowers, blooms entire season, glossy red foliage! pkt. 10c.

128 **Cactus**—Mixed; seeds from a selection of 150 choice sorts: pkt. 15c.

134 **Calceolaria**—Show mixed; gorgeous house plants, pocket-shaped flowers, profuse bloomers and rich in colors; pkt. 10c. See cut.

175 **Carnation**—Remontant or Tree; best class for winter flowers; pkt. 10c.

178 " Marguerite; blooms in three to four months from sowing seed and continues to flower almost without interruption, nearly all the blossoms come double from seeds and the marking of many sorts, are exquisite; per pkt. 10c.

205 **Cineraria**—Large-flowering, selected; one of the finest of all winter blooming plants, rare and beautiful colors; per pkt. 10c.

221 **Clianthus**—Dampieri; magnificent and curious greenhouse shrub with blazing scarlet flowers; pkt. 10c.

194 **Chrysanthemum**—Perennial or Winter Blooming sorts mixed; choice sorts of the Japanese, Chinese and Pompone in splendid mixture; per pkt. 10c.

228 **Coleus**—Show mixed; beautiful foliage of various colors, called Foliage Plant; grows well from seed; per pkt. 10c.

253 **Cyclamen**—Large-flowering, mixed; one of the most prized of all plants for a truly handsome winter bloomer; seeds sown in the spring bloom the following winter; per pkt. 10c.

316 **Fuchsia**—Show mixed; much admired house plant, grows readily from seed; pkt. 10c.

317 " Double mixed; all rare double sorts; 15 seeds 10c.

335 **Gloxinia**—Extra mixed; superb genus of plants, producing a great profusion of beautiful flowers of the richest and most brilliant colors; blooms in 6 mos. from sowing seed; pkt. 10c.

364 **Heliotrope**—Best mixed; fragrant and remains in bloom a long time; per pkt. 5c.

328 **Geranium**—Finest mixed; best known and most universally admired of all house plants; per pkt. 5c.

389 **Lantana**—Mixed; fragrant shrub plants, rich colors; pkt. 5c.

370 **Hibiscus**—Show mixed; beautiful shrubby plants, some suited for greenhouse, others hardy; pkt. 10c.

379 **Impatiens**—Sultani; House Balsam; blooms all winter; pkt 10c

565 **Primula**, or Chinese Primrose—A great winter favorite, produces lovely clusters of bloom the entire winter; 15 seeds, 10c.

567 **Primula**—Double mixed: choice double sorts; 10 seeds for 25c.

620 **Salvia**—Show mixed; called Flowering Sage; brilliant, will bloom in summer or winter; per pkt. 6c.

633 **Smilax**—Best greenhouse vine for bouquets, wreathes; pkt. 5c.

634 **Solanum**—Show mixed; beautiful fruit, ornamental; pkt. 4c.

649 **Torenia**—Charming plants for pot or vase culture; pkt. 10c.

662 **Violet**—Mixed: blooms 2nd season from seed; fragrant; pkt 10

676 **Wallflower**—Double mixed; long spikes of richly colored, fragrant flowers; per pkt. 8c.

Large packet of mixed Greenhouse Flower seeds, 25c.

Everlasting Flowers and Grasses.

Blossoms should be picked just before fully opened and dried in the shade; they will then retain their beauty for years. Grasses should be dried in a similar manner.

12 **Acroclinium**, Show Mixture; profuse bloomer, colors mostly white and pink; per pkt. 3c.

41 **Ammobium**—Free flowering, white, buds equal flowers for beauty; per pkt. 3c.

123 **Briza**, or Quaker Grass; long racemes with beautiful rattles; per pkt. 2c.

124 **Bromus**—Fine grass for winter with hanging ears; per pkt. 2c.

227 **Coix**, or Job's Tears; hanging beads, 2 feet high. (oz. 15c.); per pkt. 2c.

304 **Eragrostis**, or Love Grass; pretty, beautifully dancing spiklets; per pkt. 5c.

306 **Erianthus**—Hardy grass growing 8 to 10 ft. high, resembles pampas grass; per pkt. 5c.

311 **Eulalia**—Handsome striped hardy grass 5 to 6 ft high, resembles Ostrich Plumes; per pkt. 5c.

333 **Globe Amaranth**, or Gomphrena; pretty bloomer, resembles clover, 50 to 100 flowers on a plant; pkt. 3c

346 **Gynerium**, or Pampas Grass; magnificent silvery plumes; per pkt. 3c.

363 **Helichrysum**, Show Mixed; called Everlasting Flower, large brilliant blossoms, richly colored; pkt. 4c.

366 **Helipterum**—Clusters of bright star shaped flowers, will retain their brilliancy, fragrant; pkt. 4c.

Large packet of Everlasting Flowers and Ornamental Grass seed, mixed 10 cts.

These seeds can be sown in the open ground in spring and when large enough must be given some form of trellis or support. Those marked hardy are perennials and will stand our winters out doors.

IPOMOEA—HEAVENLY BLUE.

18—**Adlumia.** Graceful, hardy perennial climber, free bloomer and rapid grower; often called Trumpet Vine or Wood fringe Pkt. 5c.

42—**Ampelopsis Quinquefolio.** American Ivy or Woodbine. Pkt. 4c.

43—**Ampelopsis Veitchi.** Japan or Boston Ivy; one of our best hardy vines. Will cling to a smooth wall or cover a high brick building. Pkt. 5c.

117—**Bignonia Radicans.** Fine hardy climber; called Trumpet Creeper. Pkt. 5c.

152—**Canary Bird Flower.** One of the handsomest and most admired of the annual climbers; grows very rapidly and produces a profusion of canary colored blossoms resembling the expanded wings of the bird. Pkt. 5c.

181—**Celastrus.** Show Mixed. Hardy, blossoms early and is covered with scarlet berries in fall and winter. Pkt. 4c.

219—**Clematis.** Show Mixed. Many best sorts of this, the most admired of all hardy free blooming climbers. Pkt 4c.

224—**Cobaea Scandens.** Rapid grower; seed sown in May produce 20 ft. plants by August covered with large bell-shaped pendant blossoms. Pkt. 6c.

243—**Convolulus Major or Morning Glory.** Choice mixed colors. Oz. 10c. pkt. 3c.

257—**Cypress Vine.** Show Mixed. Graceful, slender vine with delicate foliage covered with bright flowers. Pkt. 3c.

1911—**Centrosema Grandiflora.** Blooms in June from seed, soon in April and is covered with a profusion of Sweet Pea like flowers 1½ to 2½ inches across of exquisite beauty. Try this if you want to see the handsomest vine you ever saw. Pkt. 15c.

299—**Dolichos or Hyacinth Bean.** Large clusters of showy flowers. Pkt. 3c.

844—**Gourds.** Choice Mixed. All sorts curious fruit. Pkt. 4c.

845—**Dish Cloth Gourd.** Lining makes elastic sponge-like durable dish cloth, also used as summer bonnet. Pkt. 8c.

881—**Ipomoea.** Leari or "Blue Dawn Flower" a rapid climber with blossoms 3 to 6 inches across. Pkt. 8c.

3012—**Ipomoea Sinuate.** Handsome, hardy vine; blooms in 2 months from seed; large white flowers with purple throat, has green capsules, large as patridge eggs; foliage beautiful. Pkt. 10c.

3013—**Ipomoea,** Heavenly Blue. Foliage large and heart shaped, blossoms 4 to 5 inches across; grows in clusters. Indescribable light blue with yellow throat. Vine always covered with these massive flowers. Pkt. 10.

388—**Japanese Hop,** Annual; ornamental species of hop, one of the best climbers for rapidly covering a window or trellis. Pkt. 5c.

429—**Moon Flower,** Blossoms 3 to 6 inches across, with Jessamine odor; climbs 25 to 40 ft. in a season; blossoms at night. Pkt. 8c.

463—**Climbing Nasturtium,** Mixed. One of the most prized climbers; blossoms very gorgeous and freely produced. Our mixture is composed of the finest sorts. Pkt. 3c, oz. 15c, ¼lb. 40c, lb. $1.25.

464—**Tropæolum Lobbianum,** Mixed Colors. One of the best Nasturtiums for house, foliage and flowers, delicate and rich. Pkt. 4c.

535—**Passiflora, or Passion Flower.** An interesting climber with singularly beautiful flowers; should have greenhouse protection in winter at the far north. Pkt. 6c.

648—**Thunbergia Mixed,** Pretty vine of slender growth; adapted to small trellises, etc. Pkt. 4c.

681—**Wistaria.** a hardy, woody climber with elegant blossoms. Pkt. 10c.

Note the low price per packet at which we mail you seed post-paid and on special discount you save one-fourth (¼) on large orders besides.

Beautiful Pansies.

We claim one of the finest strains of genuine large flowering Pansies in this country. They have been selected for years with great care and for perfection of bloom, brilliancy of color and giant flowers are not surpassed.

No.	Price per pk'g				
482	Meteor, Handsome	8	491 Silver Edge, Purple	5	502 Emperor William	5
483	Claret, Beautiful red	8	492 Gold and Bronze	5	503 Stained and Striped	5
484	King of Blacks	5	493 Mrs. Harrison, Bronze	8	504 Quadricolor	5
485	White, Pure white	5	495 Fire Dragon, Orange	5	505 Lady in White, ex. white	5
486	Pure Yellow, Golden	5	496 Rose Marbled, Beautiful	8	507 Giant Trimardeau	10
487	Dark Purple, rich color	5	497 Delicata, Light blue	5	508 Cassier's Giant Odier	10
488	Bronze, Beautiful	5	498 Odier of Blotched	10	510 Bell's English Show	8
489	Mahogany Color, Rich	5	499 Prince Bismark, Brown	5	511 Fine Mixture, (¼oz. 25c.)	5
490	Havana Brown, Showy	5	500 Lord Baconsfield	5	512 Bugnot's Large Fl'w'rn'g	10
			501 Pelargoniflora	5	787 Butterfly Pansy, Rich	10

CPSIA information can be obtained
at www.ICGtesting.com
Printed in the USA
LVHW021255071118
596294LV00004B/579